OECD Tax Policy Reviews: Chile 2022

Please cite this publication as:
OECD (2022), *OECD Tax Policy Reviews: Chile 2022*, OECD Tax Policy Reviews, OECD Publishing, Paris, https://doi.org/10.1787/0a8d9e7c-en.

ISBN 978-92-64-73593-4 (print)
ISBN 978-92-64-40817-3 (pdf)
ISBN 978-92-64-90676-1 (HTML)
ISBN 978-92-64-95008-5 (epub)

OECD Tax Policy Reviews
ISSN 2707-7691 (print)
ISSN 2707-7705 (online)

Photo credits: Cover © Marianna Ianovska/Shutterstock.com.

Corrigenda to publications may be found on line at: www.oecd.org/about/publishing/corrigenda.htm.

Foreword

This report on Chile is part of the OECD Tax Policy Reviews series. OECD Tax Policy Reviews are intended to provide independent, comprehensive and comparative assessments of OECD member and non-member countries' tax systems. By benchmarking the tax systems of countries and identifying tailored tax policy reform options, the main objective of the Reviews is to enhance the design of existing tax policies and to support the adoption and implementation of tax reforms.

The report examines the level, composition and evolution of the tax burden in Chile. In 2020, Chile's *Ministerio de Hacienda* appointed a tax commission in part to evaluate the design of the tax system in Chile. As input to this work, the OECD was commissioned by the *Ministerio de Hacienda* to undertake an independent analysis on the level, composition and evolution of the tax burden in Chile. The analysis in the report is based upon pre-COVID-19 tax revenue data up to 2019.

The report was written by Sean Kennedy with input and under the supervision from Bert Brys from the OECD Centre for Tax Policy and Administration. The authors are grateful for the support received from the Chilean Ambassador to the OECD, Mr. Francisco Saffie Gatica, as well as from Javiera Suazo, Teresa Mira and Nicolás Bohme Olivera from the *Ministerio de Hacienda*, and Mr. Rodrigo Vergara, the President of the former *Comisión Tributaria para el Crecimiento y la Equidad* in Chile. The authors would like to acknowledge the contributions of other colleagues and stakeholders in Chile who participated in discussions and provided additional information in the drafting stage of the Review.

The authors would also like to thank colleagues from the OECD Centre for Tax Policy and Administration, in particular Gioia de Melo, Michelle Harding, Michael Stemmer and David Bradbury for their helpful input and feedback, as well as Natalie Lagorce and Carrie Tyler for their assistance with typesetting and communications.

Table of contents

FIGURES

TABLES

Follow OECD Publications on:

 https://twitter.com/OECD

 https://www.facebook.com/theOECD

 https://www.linkedin.com/company/organisation-eco-cooperation-development-organisation-cooperation-developpement-eco/

 https://www.youtube.com/user/OECDiLibrary

https://www.oecd.org/newsletters/

Executive summary

This report examines the level, composition and evolution of the tax burden in Chile. The Chilean Ministry of Finance appointed a tax commission in 2020 in part to evaluate the design of the tax system in Chile. As input to this work, the OECD was commissioned by the Ministry to undertake an independent analysis on the level, composition and evolution of the tax burden in Chile. The analysis includes an examination of tax shares and income levels in Chile, the tax structure in Chile, tax convergence and a tax share path for Chile in the future.

The report is based on pre-COVID-19 tax revenue data (i.e. up to 2019). The pandemic had a significant impact on economic activity and tax revenues, either directly through the drop in economic activity or indirectly through tax measures that were taken to support the economy. It was agreed that the analysis would be based on pre-crisis revenue data so that tax revenues, the tax structure and tax convergence would not be biased by the impact of the COVID-19 pandemic. As the report was written in 2020, the tax-to-GDP data for Colombia and Costa Rica, who recently joined the OECD in 2020, are not included in the analysis in this report.

Chile's tax-to-GDP ratio is among the lowest found in the OECD, based on a range of different measures. Chile's tax-to-GDP ratio and income levels are among the lowest found in the OECD despite convergence with the OECD average over the past 30 years. Chile's tax-to-GDP ratio is lower than OECD countries when they had a similar income level to Chile (including Australia, Canada, Ireland and New Zealand). The ratio is also low when compared to the OECD average regardless of whether social security contributions (SSCs) are excluded or mandatory contributions to pension or health funds (that are managed by the private sector) are included.

Among OECD countries, Chile's tax structure is one of the most divergent from the OECD average. However, when compulsory contributions to the private sector are included in the tax-to-GDP ratio, Chile narrows the tax-to-GDP gap with the OECD average. Tax revenues in Chile are concentrated in value-added tax (VAT) and corporate income tax (CIT) while higher income OECD countries depend more on revenues from the personal income tax (PIT) and SSCs. Chile's current tax structure is also different to the tax structure in the OECD on average when GDP per capita in the OECD was closest to the current level in Chile (in the year 1978). While Chile's tax structure has converged slowly towards the OECD average tax structure over time, it has done so more slowly than other OECD countries.

The tax structure gap between Chile and the OECD is driven by VAT and PIT. When contributions to the private sector are included in SSCs, the SSC share of tax revenues in Chile is not that dissimilar to the OECD average and the absolute tax structure gap between Chile and the OECD is found to be driven by VAT and PIT. In general, tax structure gaps may point to areas that could be further explored for possible tax reform. In the case of PIT for example, the tax burden on individuals is much lower in Chile driven by a narrow PIT base and low revenues from PIT, including capital income.

The analysis in this report shows that a rising tax-to-GDP ratio over time has been the historical trend in OECD countries on average, although some countries have followed a different path. Evidence from this report supports the notion that lower tax-to-GDP ratio countries like Chile have tended to catch-up slowly with higher tax-to-GDP ratio countries over time (referred to as β-convergence). This implies that Chile may follow the path of other low tax-to-GDP ratio countries.

If Chile followed a similar path to the OECD average from when the OECD had on average a similar level of economic development to Chile's current level of GDP per capita, Chile's tax-to-GDP would be set to rise between now and 2029, but the COVID-19 pandemic has made this outcome more uncertain. To take one example, Chile's tax-to-GDP ratio is similar to Australia when Australia had a similar level of GDP per capita to Chile's current level. However, tax-to-GDP ratio growth paths are anything but guaranteed as tax-to-GDP ratios change for many reasons including tax policy choices of governments. Moreover, there may be structural elements in an economy that require differing tax levels (expenditure levels, budget deficit, public debt, dependency ratios).

Once the recovery from the COVID-19 pandemic is firmly in place, there is scope for Chile to raise its low tax level and rebalance its tax structure. The post-crisis environment will provide an opportunity for countries to undertake a more fundamental reassessment of their tax and spending policies along with their overall fiscal framework. The analysis in this report finds that few countries have reached economic prosperity historically with a low tax-to-GDP ratio. Some of the favourable demographics in Chile, which helped facilitate a low tax-to-GDP ratio, may be changing. If Chile decides to raise tax revenue, it could do so through base broadening (e.g. limiting tax expenditures rather than tax rate increases and reducing tax evasion and avoidance) and rebalancing the tax mix (e.g. by increasing personal income tax revenues, including revenues from taxes on capital income).

Summary answers to key tax policy questions facing Chile are provided below, based on the analysis in this report. This research has been developed around a series of tax policy questions relevant to Chile across different tax topics. The table below provides a summary of short answers to these questions for Chile, based on the analysis and findings in this report. The summary table has been written for clarity in a non-technical and informal way. More in-depth analysis and caveats can be found in the relevant sections indicated.

Table 1. Summary findings

Non-technical summary answers to 17 tax policy questions in Chile, by tax topic

Tax Topic	Question	Finding
A. Tax-to-GDP ratio & GDP per capita	1. At what level does Chile raise taxes? (Section 2.3)	Chile's tax-to-GDP ratio is currently among the lowest in the OECD at 20.7% in 2019 (Figure 2.2).
	2. How has Chile's GDP per capita performed relative to OECD countries? (Section 2.2)	Chile's GDP per capita income level remains relatively low, despite convergence with the OECD average over the past 30 years).
	3. When contributions to health and pension funds managed by the private sector are included, at what level does Chile raise taxes? (Section 3.4)	Chile's tax-to-GDP ratio moves closer to the OECD average to 26.9% but remains relatively low among OECD countries (Figure 3.3)
	4. Do higher income OECD countries tend to raise relatively more tax revenues? (Section 2.3)	Tax-to-GDP ratios are weakly positively correlated with income levels in the OECD, but the result is driven by outliers and there is significant heterogeneity across countries (Figure 2.3).
B. Tax structures	5. How does Chile's tax structure compare to other countries? (Section 3.1)	Chile's tax structure differs significantly from the OECD average, it is more concentrated in VAT and CIT revenues as a share of total tax revenues and less so in PIT and SSC revenues (Figure 3.1).
	6. Is Chile's tax structure becoming more or less similar to that of the OECD average? (Section 4.4)	Chile has converged with the average OECD tax structure, but more slowly than individual OECD countries have, on average, to the OECD average (Figure 4.3).
	7. At what level does Chile fund social benefits? (Section 3.2)	Chile's funding level for social benefits is relatively low. Chile's social security benefits are also financed atypically in that they are not mainly financed through SSCs, as is common in the OECD, but rather through contributions to the private sector (Figure 3.2).
	8. When compulsory contributions to the private sector are included, how does Chile's tax structure compare to OECD countries? (Section 4.4)	Chile's tax structure moves closer to the OECD average but remains among the least similar to OECD average tax structure (Figure 4.5).
	9. Which taxes drive the tax structure gap between Chile and the OECD average? (Section 4.6)	When contributions to the private sector are included in tax revenues (as are SSCs), Chile's tax structure gap with the OECD is driven by VAT and PIT and to a lesser extent CIT (Figure 4.6).
	10. How do Chile's tax rates compare to the OECD? (Section 3.5)	Tax rates on PIT, CIT and VAT in Chile and the OECD are broadly similar. This points to low tax revenues driven by a narrow tax base, particularly PIT (Table 3.2), including low tax revenues from capital income.
	11. Does the tax-to-GDP ratio grow over time in the OECD and by how much? (Section 4.1)	Tax-to-GDP ratios have tended to grow over time in the past at a rate of about 2 per cent per decade. However, tax-to-GDP in individual countries can fluctuate down and up for sustained periods (Figure 4.1).
C. Tax convergence	12. Do countries with a low tax-to-GDP ratio catch-up over time? (Section 4.2, 4.3)	Theoretical and empirical econometric evidence support the notion that low tax-to-GDP OECD countries catch-up over time (also known as tax 'beta convergence') (Figure 4.2) (Table 4.3) (1).
	13. Do lower income countries catch-up on tax-to-GDP ratio over time? (Section 4.7)	Countries with lower starting GDP per capita had faster subsequent tax-to-GDP on average, but this is not always the case (Figure 4.7).
	14. Does the evidence suggest that countries adopt policies that causes them to converge with the OECD average (tax-to-GDP ratio) over time? (Section 4.4)	The D-index suggests that the OECD may be a tax 'convergence club', which implies that lower tax-to-GDP countries like Chile may tend to converge with the OECD average over time (Figure 4.3).
D. A tax-to-GDP path for Chile	15. How does Chile's tax-to-GDP ratio compare to countries when they had similar GDP per capita to Chile? (Section 5.1)	Chile's tax-to-GDP ratio is low compared to when countries had similar levels of income (Figure 5.1). Chile's tax-to-GDP ratio is somewhat similar to Australia when Australia had a similar level of GDP per capita (Table 5.1)
	16. How might the tax-to-GDP ratio develop over the next 10 years in Chile, if it followed average OECD historical trends? (Section 5.3)	Chile's tax-to-GDP was set to rise by 2029 if it followed a similar path to the OECD average from when it had a similar level of economic development to Chile (Figure 5.3). However, the COVID-19 crisis will make this outcome much less likely.

	17. What role do demographics play in the extent to which the tax-to-GDP ratio can be raised? (Section 5.4)	Chile's low dependency ratio may have supported a lower tax level in the past, but over the coming decades the old-age dependency will rise quickly (Table 2.1).

Note: This summary table has been written in a non-technical and informal way. Technical details are available in the relevant sections in this paper. (1) The beta convergence estimate is based on OECD countries only over the period 1965 to 2019.

Table 2. Key measures in Chile and the OECD

	Chile	OECD
Tax-to-GDP ratio measures		
Tax-to-GDP ratio (2019)	20.7% (18.3% in 1990)	33.8% (32.5% in 1990)
Tax-to-GDP growth since 1995	2.4 pp	1.3 pp
Income & demographic measures		
GDP per capita, USD	23,151 (12,253 in 1990)	42,953 (29,921 in 1990)
Old-age dependency ratio in 2025	23.6 (43.0 in 2050)	35.2 (53.2 in 2050)
Tax mix measures		
VAT-to-revenue ratio	39.9%	20.4%
CIT-to-revenue ratio	23.4%	10.0%
PIT-to-revenue ratio	1.5%	8.1%
SSC-to-revenue ratio	1.5%	9.0%
Compulsory contributions to private sector	5.8%	0.9%
Selected tax rates		
Top PIT rate	40.0%	42.8%
Standard VAT rate	19.0%	19.3%
CIT rate	25.0%	23.5%
Tax convergence		
Sigma convergence (D-index*)	74.5 (79.5 in 1990)	34.5 (44.3 in 1990)
Sigma convergence (adjusted D-index*)	59.9 (69.8 in 1990)	33.3 (37.5 in 1990)
Other tax-to-GDP ratio measures		
Tax-to-GDP ratio (excluding SSCs), 2018	19.6%	24.3%
Tax-to-GDP ratio (including compulsory contributions to the private sector)	26.9%	34.8%

Note: Information related to the data sources and calculations for the figures provided in this table are provided throughout this report.
*In the case of the D-index, the OECD average is calculated as the mean average of the sum of the absolute differences in all OECD countries, which provides an indicator of the extent to which tax structures are different or similar across countries in the OECD.
Source: OECD (2020), Revenue Statistics 2020, OECD Publishing, Paris, https://doi.org/10.1787/8625f8e5-en, OECD (2019), OECD Compendium of Productivity Indicators 2019, OECD Publishing, Paris, https://doi.org/10.1787/b2774f97-en.; OECD tax database statistics; United Nations, World Population Prospects – 2017 Revision; OECD calculations.

1 Introduction

This chapter provides some background to the project in addition to the data and methodology used. It also describes the structure of the report.

Background and methodology

This objective of this research is to examine the level, composition and evolution of the tax burden in Chile. The Chilean Ministry of Finance appointed a tax commission in 2020 in part to evaluate the design of the tax system in Chile. As input to this work, the OECD was commissioned by the Ministry to undertake an independent analysis on the level, composition and evolution of the tax burden in Chile. The analysis includes an examination of tax shares and income levels in Chile, tax structure in Chile, tax convergence and a tax share path for Chile in the future.

The two main measures used in this research are the tax-to-GDP ratio and GDP per capita. This report uses two main measures. The first measure is the tax-to-GDP ratio, defined according to *OECD Revenue Statistics*. SSCs are classified as taxes[1]. The data is arranged by year and country. The second measure is income or GDP per capita. For the purposes of this report, GDP per capita is defined as GDP per capita in USD, measured in 2015 Purchasing Power Parities (PPP[2]). Given the focus on the tax-to-GDP ratio in this report, it is worth mentioning the concept of tax buoyancy whereby an increase in economic activity, measured by GDP, may in itself produce increases in tax revenue. For example, a tax buoyancy of one would imply that an increase in GDP of one percent would increase tax revenue by one percent, meaning that the tax-to-GDP ratio would remain unchanged. A tax buoyancy above one would mean that tax revenues would rise faster than GDP causing the tax-to-GDP ratio to rise. Empirical evidence based on OECD countries has found that in the short-run buoyancy is close to one for the majority of OECD countries and in the long-run buoyancy is not significantly different from one in about half of the OECD countries (Belinga et al., 2014[1]).

SSCs in Chile are private and therefore not considered to be taxes under the OECD definition. In Chile, mandatory contributions to pension or health funds are managed by the private sector. These funds are not classified as SSCs under the above OECD definition. Consequently, SSCs in Chile appear relatively lower based on the OECD definition than they would if mandatory contributions to the private sector were included. To enhance the comparison of the tax-to-GDP ratio in Chile and the OECD as part of this report, mandatory contributions to the private sector are included in SSCs (see Section 2.2 for further discussion). Furthermore, Chile's social security benefits are not mainly financed through SSCs, as is common in the OECD, but rather through contributions to the private sector (see Section 3.2).

OECD data are the main data source used for analysis, particularly OECD revenue statistics data. This report draws primarily on tax-to-GDP ratio data for Chile and OECD countries between 1965 and 2019 based on *OECD Revenue Statistics* data (OECD, 2020[2]). Tax-to-GDP data for Colombia and Costa Rica, who recently joined the OECD in 2020, are not included in the analysis in this report. While 2019 represents the most up-to-date year of available data, it should be noted that tax revenues declined in Chile in 2019 partly due to social unrest. The report also uses revenue statistics data and analysis on the financing of social security benefits from the revenue statistics memorandum tables (OECD, 2020[2]). OECD global revenue statistics data are also used. GDP per capita data are also used for Chile and OECD countries in the OECD compendium of productivity statistics between 1970 and 2019.

Tax-to-GDP ratios evolve for a complex set of economic, demographic and social reasons and policy choices. The current study provides a range of statistical analysis on the development and possible future trajectory of the tax level and tax structure in Chile compared to OECD and other countries. However, the tax level in a country (measured by the tax-to-GDP ratio) and the tax structure (measured by tax categories as a share of total tax revenues) vary between and within countries over time for a complex set of historical, economic, demographic, social and political reasons (OECD, 2018[3]). Some of these reasons relate to policy choices on taxation and welfare. In recent decades, tax structures in OECD countries have changed, notably there has been a shift away from personal income taxes and non-VAT consumption taxes, toward higher SSCs. Furthermore, OECD research has found that that different taxes affect growth differently (OECD, 2010[4]) and this may have contributed to policy decisions on tax structure in some OECD countries.

GDP per capita in PPP is only one measure of economic growth. In the present research, economic growth is measured using GDP per capita in PPP. However, other measures could have been used (nominal GDP growth, GDP real growth, GDP PPP growth), which would in turn have implications for the measurement of convergence. Since 1980, Chile's population growth (68% in total) has expanded at more than double the rate in the OECD (32%) (Chile's population grew from 11.1 million in 1980 to 18.8 million in 2018)[3]. Consequently, compared to using GDP as a measure, GDP per capita growth will be lower in Chile due to its faster population growth (holding other factors constant).

A set of comparison countries are used in this research. For the purposes of the report, a number of comparison countries are used. First, the OECD average is used[4]. From a methodological perspective, the OECD average can be calculated based on a different number of countries in different years because new countries join the OECD over time. Furthermore, newer joiners have tended to be relatively less developed which also has implications for statistical averages. Second, the Latin American and Caribbean (LAC) country average is also used and similar methodological issues apply. Third, four comparison countries were chosen by Chile, namely, Australia, Canada, Ireland and New Zealand. Finally, a number of resource-rich countries are chosen, namely, Canada, Brazil, Norway and Mexico.

Different measures of tax convergence are measured empirically (Section 4). In the field of economics, convergence generally refers to economic convergence, which can be defined as low-income economies closing the gap with richer economies over time (measured using GDP per capita). Tax convergence is a similar concept which implies that lower tax-to-GDP ratio countries (such as Chile) catch-up with higher tax-to-GDP ratio countries over time. There are two commonly adopted approaches to measure tax convergence:

1. β tax convergence tells us whether low-tax countries catch-up (in terms of their tax-to-GDP ratio) with high-tax countries over time;
2. σ tax convergence occurs in a group of countries when there is a decline in the dispersion of the tax-to-GDP ratio over time.

Tax convergence can be measured empirically using correlational and econometric analysis.

Structure

The report contains four chapters focusing on different tax topics in Chile: tax revenues and income levels, tax structure, tax convergence and a tax-to-GDP ratio path for the future. Chapter 2 evaluates Chile's tax-to-GDP ratio and GDP per capita compared to the OECD and comparison countries in recent decades. It also examines the relationship between tax-to-GDP and GDP per capita generally and the extent to which Chile has converged with the average of OECD countries over time. Chapter 3 compares the tax structure in Chile with the OECD average. The Chapter also considers the role of some relatively atypical features of the tax structure in Chile including Social Security Contributions and compulsory contributions to the private sector. Selected tax rates in Chile are also compared with the OECD average to add context to the tax structure discussion. Chapter 4 begins by considering the historical growth pattern of tax-to-GDP in OECD countries. The chapter then examines theoretical and empirical evidence for whether low tax-to-GDP countries catch-up with high tax-to-GDP countries over time (known as beta tax convergence) and whether Chile's tax structure has become more similar to the OECD average over time (known as sigma tax convergence). Lastly, it measures Chile's tax structure similarity to the OECD average and identifies the largest absolute tax differences, which provide a starting point for identifying areas of potential tax reform. Chapter 5 begins by comparing Chile's tax-to-GDP ratio with countries when they had similar levels of economic development. It then projects a possible tax-to-GDP path for Chile over the coming decade if it were to follow the path of countries from when they had a similar level of economic development. The Chapter also highlights how some of the favourable demographics in Chile contributed to a low tax-to-GDP ratio are shifting.

2 Tax revenues and income levels

This chapter evaluates Chile's tax-to-GDP ratio and GDP per capita compared to the OECD and comparison countries in recent decades. It also examines the relationship between tax-to-GDP and GDP per capita generally and the extent to which Chile has converged with the average of OECD countries over time.

Chile's GDP per capita remains relatively low, despite its relative convergence with the OECD average over the past 30 years

Some evidence supports that GDP per capita convergence occurs at 2% yearly. GDP per capita convergence, often described as the catch-up process, refers to the process by which less advanced economies with lower-income per capita converge towards more advanced economies through higher growth rates, as they capitalise on technology transfer, inward investment, and relatively lower labour costs. Some long-term empirical evidence supports a convergence hypothesis at a speed of 2% annually (Young, Higgins, Levy, 2004), although counter evidence also exists (see Monfort, 2008).

Chile's GDP per capita has grown at a 2.7% annually since 1995, faster than OECD average rate. Chile's GDP per capita was USD 12 253 (in 2015 PPP) in 1995 and USD 23,151 in 2019, which represents a compound annual growth rate (CAGR) of 2.7% over the period (see Figure 2.1). Over the same period, the OECD average GDP per capita was USD 29 921 in 1995 and USD 42 953 in 2019, which represents a CAGR of 1.5%. As a result, Chile's GDP per capita converged with the OECD average over the period – GDP per capita in Chile represented 41% of the OECD average in 1995 but 54% in 2019. GDP per capita in Chile grew faster than the OECD average over the period, albeit the rate of growth was somewhat slower after 2007. Since 2007, Chile's GDP per capita has grown by a CAGR of 1.7% compared to 0.9% in the OECD. Over the full period 1995 to 2019, Chile has experienced relative convergence with the OECD average, albeit it has not experienced absolute convergence (i.e. the absolute income gap between Chile and the OECD has not decreased during the period). For a discussion of relative and absolute convergence, see (Kant, 2019[5]).

Figure 2.1. Chile's GDP per capita has grown faster than the OECD average

GDP per capita in Chile and the OECD, USD constant prices (2015 PPP), 1995 - 2019

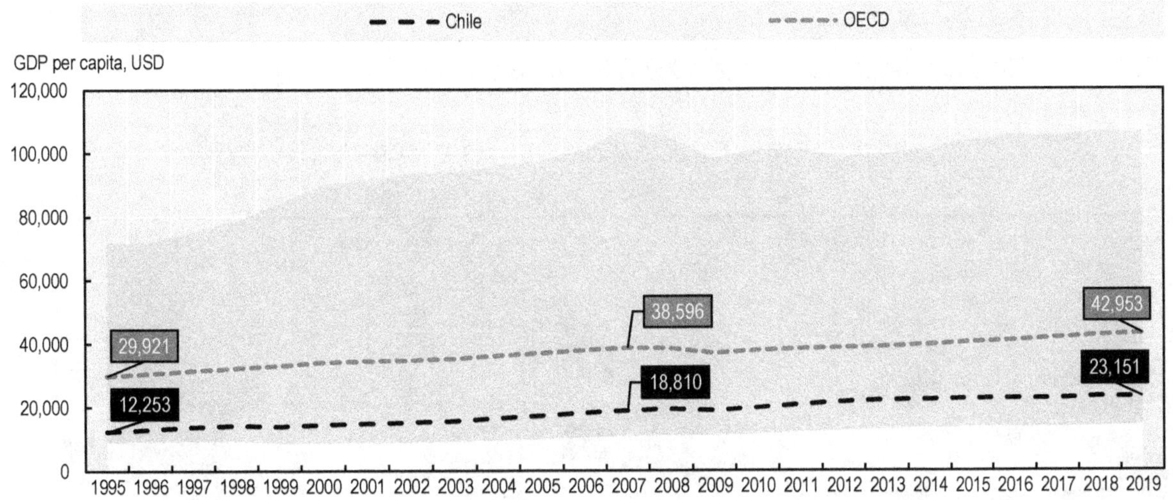

Source: OECD (2019), OECD Compendium of Productivity Indicators 2019, OECD Publishing, Paris, https://doi.org/10.1787/b2774f97-en.

Chile's tax-to-GDP remains among the lowest in the OECD, despite its convergence with the OECD over recent years

Chile's current tax-to-GDP ratio is among the lowest found in OECD countries and it has been consistently lower than the OECD average over the past 30 years. In 2019, the latest year for which data are available,

Chile's tax-to-GDP ratio is 20.7% compared to 33.8% in the OECD. Since 1995, Chile's tax-to-GDP ratio has been consistently below the OECD average, as shown in Figure 2.2.

Chile's tax-to-GDP ratio had been converging with the OECD average up to its peak in 2007, but it has been diverging since then. As shown in Figure 2.2, the tax-to-GDP ratio in Chile increased from 18.3% in 1995 to 20.7% in 2019, an increase of 2.4 percentage points. Over the same period, the tax-to-GDP ratio in OECD countries increased from 32.5% in 1995 to 33.8% in 2019, an increase of 1.3 percentage points. As a result of Chile's faster tax-to-GDP growth rate over the period, Chile's tax-to-GDP ratio as a share of the OECD tax-to-GDP ratio has caught up or converged with the OECD, increasing from 56% in 1995 to 61% in 2019. However, a reversal in the pattern of the tax-to-GDP ratio emerges when the time period is split in to two equal length periods (of 12 years). In the first period from 1995 to 2007, Chile's tax-to-GDP ratio converged with the OECD average – it grew by 4.4 percentage points in total compared to 0.7 percentage points in the OECD. In the second period from 2007 to 2019, Chile's tax-to-GDP ratio diverged with the OECD average, it declined by 2.1 percentage points while the OECD average continued to grow at 0.7percentage points (the same rate as the previous period). Overall, Chile's tax-to-GDP ratio rose and grew faster than the OECD average between 1995 and 2007 (causing convergence) but has declined and grown relatively slower than the OECD average since then (causing divergence).

The relatively high volatility of Chile's tax-to-GDP ratio and its divergence from the OECD average after 2007 was partly driven by fluctuations in tax revenues from copper mining. The tax-to-GDP ratio in Chile has also been more volatile than the OECD average, partly due to tax revenues from resources such as mining. For example, the increase in the tax-to-GDP ratio in the mid-2000s was partly driven by copper revenues, which rose dramatically from 1.0% in 2003 to 8.1% in 2007 (OECD, 2018[6]). If tax revenues from copper were excluded, the tax-to-GDP ratio would have been closer to 17.3% in 2007, rather than 22.7%[5]. Therefore, much of the rapid tax-to-GDP ratio convergence in Chile with the OECD average up to 2007 can be attributed to tax revenues from copper mining.

Figure 2.2. Chile's tax-to-GDP ratio had been converging with the OECD average up to its peak in 2007, but it has been diverging since then

Tax-to-GDP ratio in Chile and the OECD average, 1990 - 2019 as % of GDP

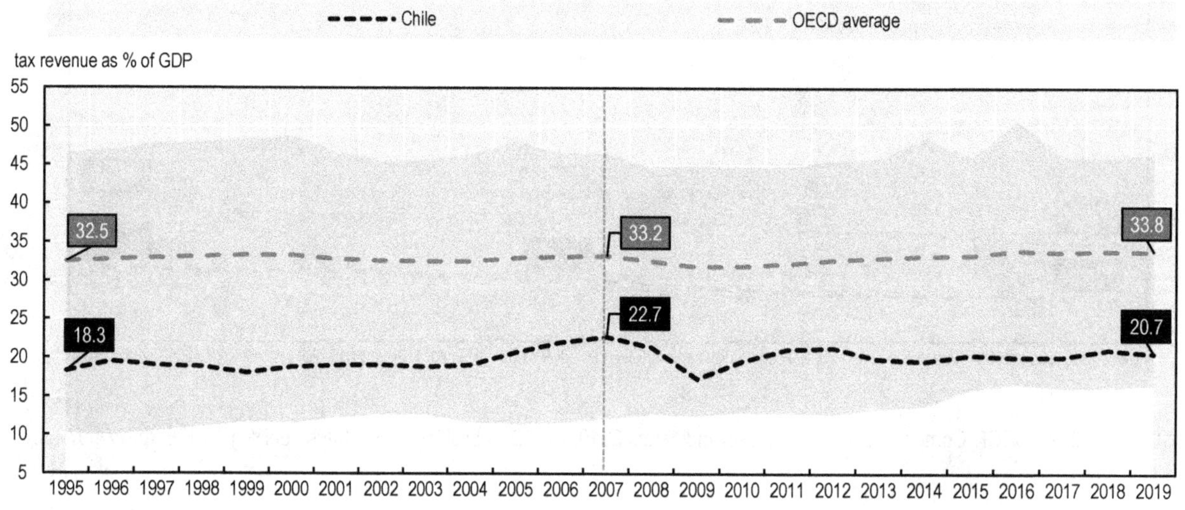

Note: The grey shaded area shows the maximum and minimum tax-to-GDP ratios in OECD countries in each year. OECD average SSC data for 2019 are not available so 2018 data is used.
Source: OECD (2020), Revenue Statistics 2020, OECD Publishing, Paris, https://doi.org/10.1787/8625f8e5-en

Chile's tax-to-GDP ratio has been growing at about 1 percentage point a decade. Between 1995 and 2019, and on an average annual basis, the tax-to-GDP ratio increased in Chile and the OECD by 0.10 and 0.05 percentage points, respectively. By extension then, over ten years the tax-to-GDP ratio grew by roughly 1 percentage point compared to 0.54 percentage points in the OECD.

When SSCs are excluded from tax revenues, the tax-to-GDP gap between Chile and OECD is narrowed due to the relatively small role played by SSCs in Chile. The OECD classifies SSCs as tax revenues[6], which play a large role in most OECD countries but a much smaller role in Chile. In 2019, SSCs as a share of GDP were 1.5% in Chile, compared to 9.0% in the OECD. Relative to the size of the economy then, SSC revenues are about six times greater in the OECD average than in Chile. This large difference in the importance of SSC revenues has implications for the tax-to-GDP gap between Chile and the OECD average. Figure 2.1 shows that when SSCs are excluded from tax revenues, Chile's tax-to-GDP ratio is much more similar to the OECD average. In 2019 for example, when SSCs are included in tax revenues the tax-to-GDP gap between Chile and the OECD is 13.2 percentage points compared to just 5.3 percentage points when SSCs are excluded[7]. Furthermore, when SSCs are excluded, the tax-to-GDP ratio has also been converging more quickly with the OECD average over time. When SSCs are excluded, the gap between Chile and the OECD was 8.6 percentage points in 1990 and 5.3 in 2019 compared to 14.2 in 1990 and 13.2 when SSCs are included. However, it has to be pointed out that excluding SSCs from the tax-to-GDP ratio represents an unorthodox analytical approach, which may not be very informative and could even be misleading. This is particularly the case because SSCs play a significant and growing role in the tax revenues of many OECD countries and have been growing as a share of tax revenues in OECD countries in recent decades. Indeed, from the taxpayer's perspective, it may be more insightful to measure the total mandatory burden, including all taxes (including SSC) and compulsory contributions to the private sector. The extent of convergence between Chile and the OECD when compulsory payments to the private sector are included is provided later in the report in Section 3.3.

Despite Chile's faster growth relative to the Latin American and Caribbean countries average, Chile's tax-to-GDP ratio grew more slowly. Figure 2.1 shows the tax-to-GDP ratio and GDP per capita in Chile and Latin American and Caribbean (LAC) countries between 1990 and 2018. According to the analysis, Chile's income has increased faster than the Latin American and Caribbean (LAC) countries on average, but its tax-to-GDP ratio has grown more slowly.

Table 2.1. Chile's tax-to-GDP ratio grew more slowly than the LAC average since 1990

Changes in tax-to-GDP ratio and GDP per capita in Chile and Latin American and Caribbean, 1990 - 2018

	GDP per capita in USD (in PPP)			Tax-to-GDP ratio		
	1990	2018	Annual change (in % CAGR)	1990	2018	Total change (in pp)
Chile	4,511	24,765	6.3%	16.9	21.1	4.2
LAC	5,542	16,396	4.0%	15.9	23.1	7.1

Note: GDP per capita, in USD, in PPP. PP refers to percentage points. LAC average represents the group of 25 Latin American and Caribbean countries in the OECD Revenue Statistics in Latin America and the Caribbean publication and excludes Venezuela due to data availability issues.
Source: OECD (2020), Revenue Statistics 2020, OECD Publishing, Paris, https://doi.org/10.1787/8625f8e5-en and World Bank development indicators database.

Tax-to-GDP ratios are weakly positively correlated with income levels, but there is significant heterogeneity across countries and outliers drive the relationship

Chile's current tax-to-GDP ratio is not just low relative to most OECD countries today but it is low relative to most OECD countries in any given year over the past half century. In the previous section, it was established that Chile's GDP per capita and tax-to-GDP ratio grew faster than the OECD average in recent decades. This finding is also confirmed in Figure 2.3, where the tax-to-GDP ratio is highlighted for Chile in 1990 and 2019 and in the OECD in 1965 and 2019. Chile's 2019 tax-to-GDP ratio of 20.7% is relatively low compared not just to OECD countries in 2019 but also to OECD countries in any year over the past half century. Chile's overall tax-to-GDP ratio and income is not so different from the OECD's in 1965 (however, its tax structure is different, as we see in the next section). The tax-to-GDP ratio does not include compulsory payments to private sector funds, which are explored later in the report (see Section 3.3).

Few countries have reached a high level of economic prosperity with a low-tax-to-GDP ratio. Countries that have had economic prosperity have also tended to have high tax-to-GDP ratios. Countries that have had economic prosperity with a low tax-to-GDP are among the minority. One example is Ireland, shown in bottom right of the chart.

Tax-to-GDP ratios have had a historical upper bound of about 50% of GDP. Over more than half a century of data, the tax-to-GDP ratio has never risen above 50% (the maximum tax-to-GDP for any OECD country in any year was 48.9%).

Tax-to-GDP ratios are positively correlated with GDP per capita, but there is significant heterogeneity. Figure 2.3 shows the relationship between tax-to-GDP and GDP per capita in OECD countries in all years between 1965 and 2019. The data shows a weakly positive relationship between tax-to-GDP ratio and GDP per capita, with a few outlying countries driving the relationship.

Figure 2.3. Tax-to-GDP ratios are positively correlated with income, but there is significant heterogeneity

Relationship between tax-to-GDP and GDP per capita in OECD countries, all years 1965 - 2019

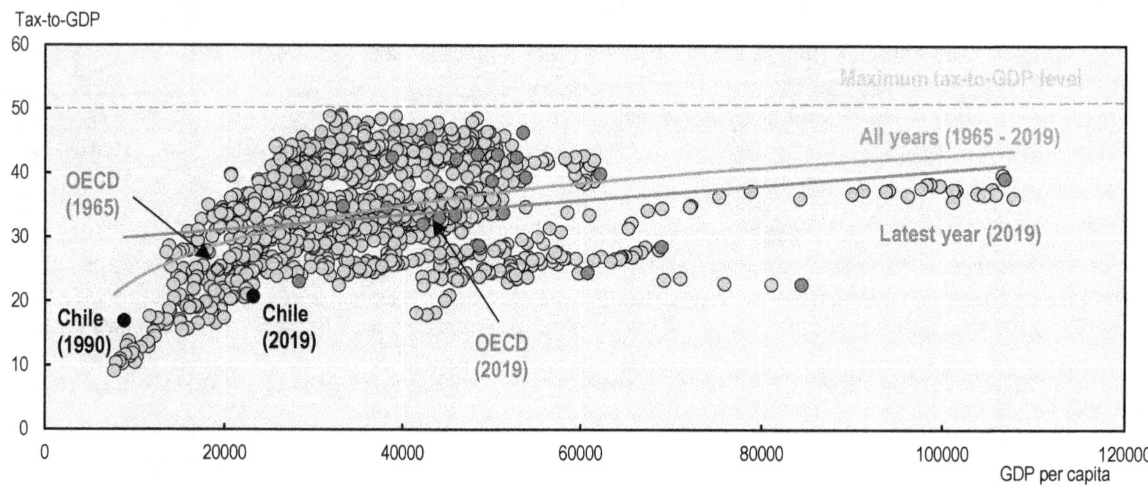

Note: Only OECD countries where data are available for all years 1965 to 2019 are shown.
Source: OECD (2020), Revenue Statistics 2020, OECD Publishing, Paris, https://doi.org/10.1787/8625f8e5-en and OECD Compendium of Productivity Indicators 2019, OECD Publishing, Paris, https://doi.org/10.1787/b2774f97-en

However, group averages mask heterogeneity and a range of tax-to-GDP ratios paths are possible within individual countries. An abundance of natural resources, but not a dependence on them, can be positive for growth, and can be positive for tax revenues, if receipts are invested rather than consumed (OECD, 2006[7]). Figure 2.4 compares Chile to selected resource-rich and comparison countries (defined in Chapter 1) between 1990 and 2018. Resource-rich oil countries have a wide range of tax-to-GDP ratios – in 2018, from Norway (39.6% of GDP) to Brazil (33.1%) to Mexico (16.1%). The selected comparison countries have a narrower range – in 2018, from Canada (32.9%) to Ireland (22.3%). Chile's tax-to-GDP ratio is the lowest compared to the comparison countries and the lowest compared to the resource-rich countries, with the exception of Mexico. Figure 2.4 also highlights how tax-to-GDP ratios follow a wide range of different paths over time and can rise or fall for sustained periods of time reflecting economic conditions in the country.

Figure 2.4. Chile's tax-to-GDP ratio is relatively low compared to selected comparison and resource-rich countries

Tax-to-GDP ratios, Chile, selected comparison countries and resource-rich countries, 1990 - 2018

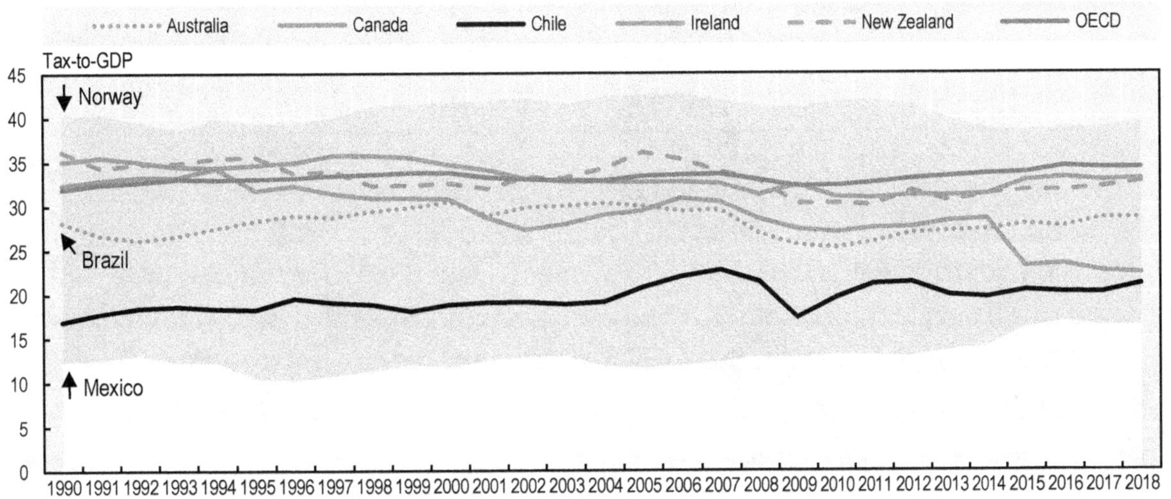

Note: Comparison countries are Australia, Canada, Ireland and New Zealand. Resource-rich countries are Norway, Mexico and Brazil. Canada is not included as a resource-rich country as it is already used as a comparison country.
Source: OECD (2020), Revenue Statistics 2020, OECD Publishing, Paris, https://doi.org/10.1787/8625f8e5-en.

3 Tax structures

This chapter compares the tax structure in Chile with the OECD average. The chapter also considers the role of some relatively atypical features of the tax structure in Chile including Social Security Contributions and compulsory contributions to the private sector. Selected tax rates in Chile are also compared with the OECD average to add context to the tax structure discussion.

Chile's tax structure differs significantly from the OECD average, it is more concentrated in VAT and CIT revenues and less so in PIT and SSC revenues

Tax revenues in Chile are relatively low. Chile's tax-to-GDP was 20.7% in 2019, substantially below the OECD average rate of 33.8% in 2019 (33.9% in 2018). Consequently, relative to the size of its economy (measured by GDP), Chile raises tax revenues of about 60% of the OECD average.

Tax revenues in Chile are concentrated in VAT and CIT. As shown in Figure 3.1, taxes on goods and services represent over half of total tax revenues (53.1%) in Chile in 2019, compared to about one-third (32.7%) in the OECD in 2018 (VAT represents 39.9% of total tax revenues in Chile, compared to 20.4% in the OECD). CIT revenues as a share of total tax revenues were 23.4% in Chile in 2019, compared to 10% among OECD countries. Combined, VAT and CIT revenues in Chile represent more than three-quarters of total tax revenues, compared to less than half among OECD countries. When compared as a share of GDP, VAT and CIT in Chile were 8.2% and 4.8% respectively in 2019, which are both above the OECD average of 6.8% and 3.1% in 2018. On the other hand, PIT and SSCs and taxes on payroll play a much smaller role in Chile. For example, PIT and SSCs as a share of GDP in Chile both represent 1.5% in 2019, which is significantly below the OECD average of 8.1% and 9.0% respectively in 2018. Higher income OECD countries generally depend more heavily on PIT and SSCs than in Chile. Chile's relatively high concentration in CIT and relatively low concentration in PIT has various causes, including Chile's partial dividend imputation tax system under which the CIT that is withheld at source is partially credited against the PIT when dividends are distributed (see also (OECD, 2020[8])).

Chile's tax mix was different to the OECD average (and more different than currently) when the OECD had similar GDP per capita to Chile in 1978. Chile's GDP per capita is USD 23 151 in 2019, significantly below the OECD average of USD 42 953. It is instructive to compare Chile's tax mix to the OECD at the time when the OECD was economically more similar to Chile. The OECD's GDP per capita was most similar to Chile's current GDP per capita in the year 1978, when it was USD 22 994. Despite a more similar income level, Chile's tax mix is actually less similar to the OECD average in 1978 than it is to the OECD in 2018, as shown in Figure 3.1.

Figure 3.1. Chile's tax revenues are relatively concentrated in VAT and CIT

Tax revenues in Chile and the OECD, 2018 and 1978 (the year in which the OECD had a similar GDP per capita to Chile)

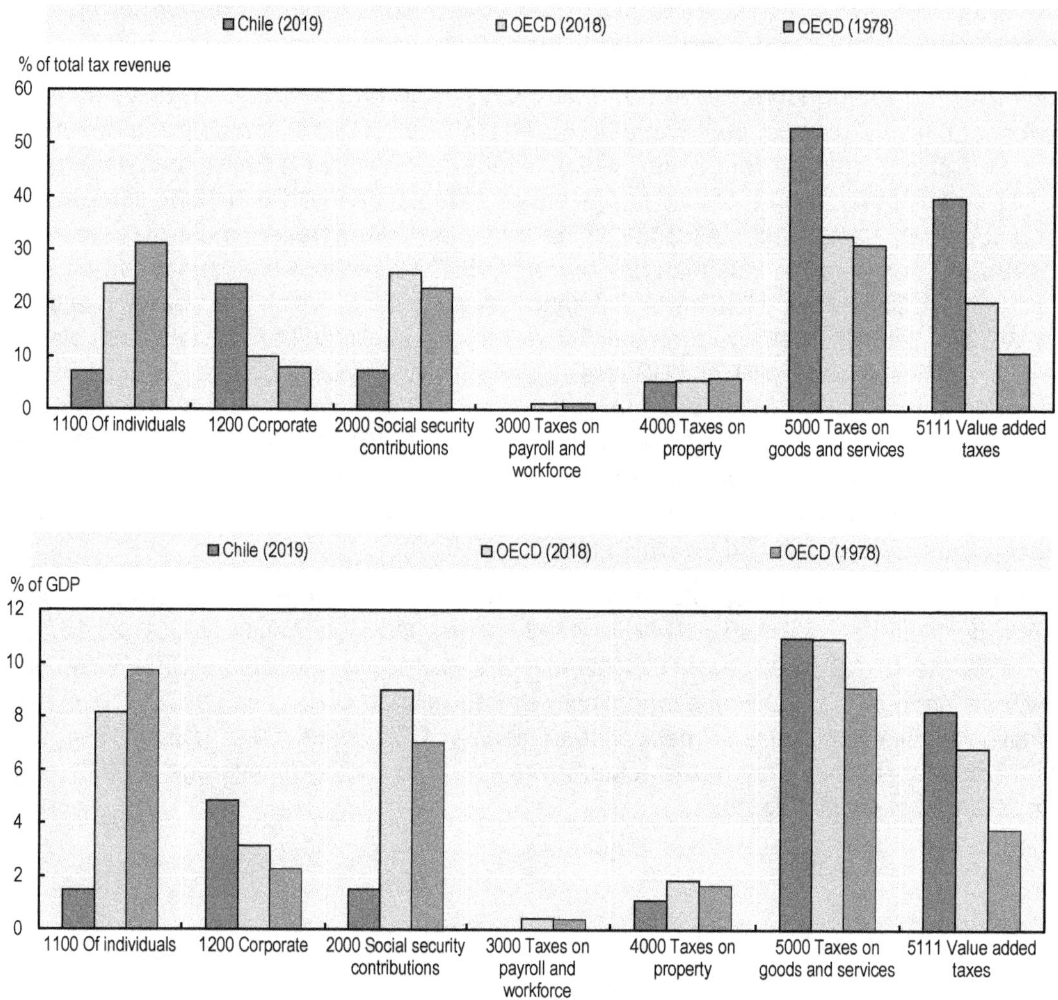

Note: OECD average data is for the year 2018 as this is the latest available data by tax categories. For Chile and the OECD average, the taxes shown represent 96.4% and 98.7% of total taxes respectively. Since Chile's tax-to-GDP ratio (20.7%) is below the OECD average (33.8%) in 2019, the tax-to-GDP figures by tax category in Chile are relatively smaller than taxes as a share of total tax revenues.
Source: OECD (2020), Revenue Statistics 2020, OECD Publishing, Paris, https://doi.org/10.1787/8625f8e5-en.

Some aspects of Chile's tax structure are atypical such as the small role of SSCs and the large role of compulsory contributions to the private sector

Social benefits are mostly funded by SSCs in the OECD, but other funding sources exist. Social benefits provided by governments require funding. The most common source of financing for social security-type benefits in OECD countries are taxes, and for the most part SSCs. SSCs along with other earmarked taxes account for over 90% of the financing of social security-type benefits in 25 OECD countries and 100% in 13 countries (OECD, 2020[2]). SSCs are usually paid to the government and used to provide a social benefit (or contingent entitlement) in the future. Examples include unemployment benefit (in the event an individual loses her employment) and child benefit (in the event an individual has a child).

In addition to SSCs, social benefits can also be financed with a number of other sources, as shown in Figure 3.1. SSCs and other taxes earmarked for social security-type benefits represent tax revenues sources. Voluntary contributions to governments and compulsory contributions to the private sector represent non-tax revenues sources.

Chile's social security benefits are not mainly financed through SSCs, as is common in the OECD, but rather through contributions to the private sector. According to the analysis in Figure 3.1, Chile's overall finances for social benefits is relatively small (7.2% of GDP) compared to the OECD average (11.1% of GDP). Chile's social benefits financing is also highly concentrated in non-tax revenues, specifically compulsory contributions to the private sector (5.8%), relative to the OECD average (0.9% of GDP). It follows that Chile's social benefits financing is not particularly focused on taxes, especially SSCs (1.5% of GDP), relative to the OECD average (9.5% of GDP).

Table 3.1. Chile's social security benefits are mostly financed by contributions to the private sector

Financing sources for social security-type benefits in Chile and the OECD, 2018

Tax and non-tax	Source	Chile (% of GDP)	OECD average* (% of GDP)
Tax revenues	1. Social security contributions (SSCs)	1.5	9.5
	2. Other taxes earmarked for social security-type benefits	0	0.6
Non-tax revenues	3. Voluntary contributions to government	0	0.1
	4. Compulsory contributions to private sector	5.8	0.9
Total		**7.2**	**11.1**

Note: *The OECD average is calculated as weighted average for countries where data are available and does not include Australia, New Zealand and the Netherlands. Further details relating to the caveats are available in the source below.
Source: OECD (2020), Revenue Statistics 2020, OECD Publishing, Paris, https://doi.org/10.1787/8625f8e5-en.

Compulsory contributions to the private sector play a role in several OECD countries

Contributions to the private sector are very significant in Chile, and far more so than SSCs. In Chile, the tax-to-GDP ratio is 21.1% in 2018 and compulsory contributions to the private sector represent a significant 5.8% of GDP in 2018 or 27.5% of total tax revenues. By comparison, SSCs represent 1.5% of GDP or 6.9% of tax revenues in Chile in 2018. Therefore, compulsory contributions to the private sector are a factor of four times larger than SSCs in Chile.

Compulsory contributions to the private sector are important for financing social security benefits in several OECD countries including Chile. Figure 3.2 shows that SSCs provide the largest source of financing for social security-type benefits in most OECD countries. In Chile, compulsory contributions to the private sector play a significant role, representing 79.6% of total SSCs. Compulsory payments to the private similar sector also play a significant role in other OECD countries including Colombia (68.6%), Switzerland (52.7%) and Iceland (46.1%) and to a lesser extent in Mexico (34.6%) and Israel (34.2%).

Figure 3.2. Compulsory contributions to the private sector play a role in several OECD countries

Financing of social security benefits, % of GDP, 2018

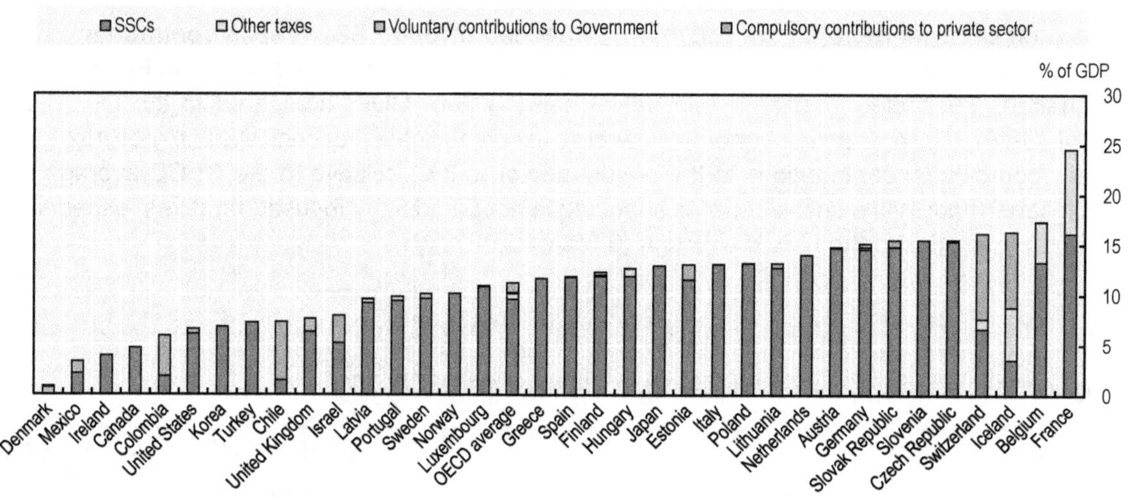

Source: OECD (2020), Revenue Statistics 2020, OECD Publishing, Paris, https://doi.org/10.1787/8625f8e5-en.

Chile's tax-to-GDP ratio remains relatively low, regardless of whether SSCs are excluded or contributions to private sector are included

When compulsory contributions to the private sector are included, Chile's tax-to-GDP ratio ranking among OECD countries changes from the 3rd lowest to the 7th lowest. As noted previously, Figure 3.3 shows that Chile's tax-to-GDP ratio is significantly below the OECD average (21.1% in 2018 compared to 33.7% in the OECD). Indeed, Chile's tax-to-GDP was the 3rd lowest in the OECD in 2018. Some commentators might argue that tax-to-GDP comparisons with the OECD are misleading given Chile's atypically low SSC revenues and large compulsory contributions from the private sector. However, drawing a tax-to-GDP comparison in the OECD by excluding SSCs has the potential to be misleading because SSCs play a significant role in the tax revenues of many OECD countries and SSCs as a share of tax revenues have increased in OECD countries in recent decades. Similarly, adding compulsory contributions to the private sector to the tax-to-GDP share is not considered standard practice in the OECD. Notwithstanding these caveats, Figure 3.3 shows the tax-to-GDP ratio in Chile and OECD countries without SSCs and alternatively with contributions to the private sector. Three main results are obtained. First, when SSCs and other earmarked taxes are excluded from the analysis, Chile's tax-to-GDP narrows the gap with the OECD average (19.6% compared to 24.3% in 2018 respectively) but remains among the lower tax-to-GDP countries in the OECD (9th lowest). Second, when SSCs are excluded, Chile's tax to-GDP ratio is only modestly below that of the OECD average of 23% in 1978 when the OECD had a similar level of economic development to Chile's current level (see Chapter 5 for a further exploration of this analytical approach). Third, when compulsory contributions from the private sector are included in the analysis, Chile's tax-to-GDP similarly moves closer to the OECD average (26.9% compared to 34.7% in 2018 respectively). Once again however, Chile remains among the lowest tax-to-GDP countries in the OECD (7th lowest).

Figure 3.3. Chile's tax-to-GDP ratio remains relatively low without SSCs and with private contributions

Tax-to-GDP ratios and financing of social security type benefits, % of GDP, 2018

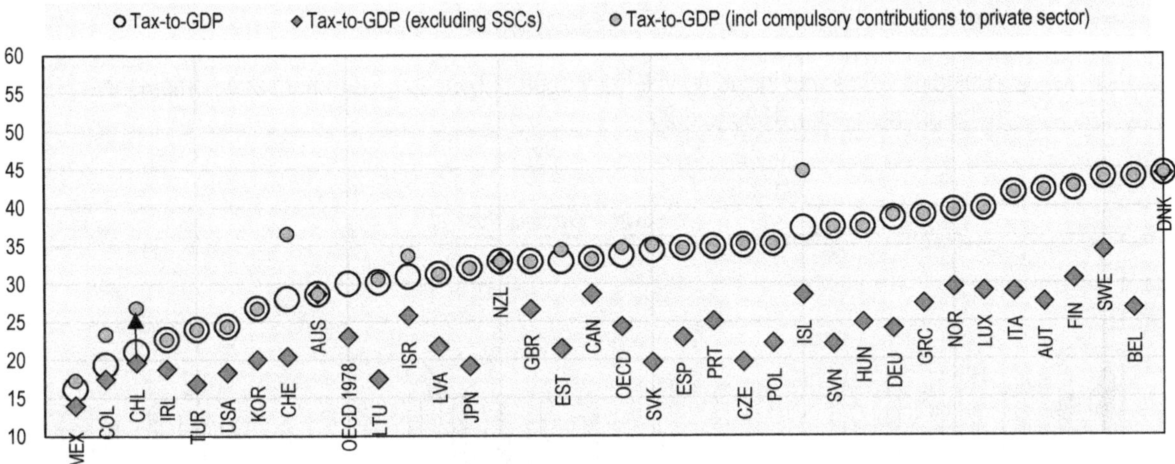

Note: The tax-to-GDP ratio (excluding SSCs) refers to excluding SSCs and also other earmarked taxes. The Netherlands are not included in the figure as complete data on social security financing were not available.
Source: OECD (2020), Revenue Statistics 2020, OECD Publishing, Paris, https://doi.org/10.1787/8625f8e5-en.

Since 1990, Chile narrowed the tax-to-GDP gap with the OECD relatively faster when the tax-to-GDP is adjusted to account for Chile's atypical tax structure

Between 1990 and 2019, Chile's tax-to-GDP narrowed the gap with the OECD average by 1.1 percentage points, when no adjustments are made to the tax-to-GDP ratio. This section examines the development of the tax-to-GDP ratio in Chile and OECD countries over time in 1990 and 2018 (Figure 3.4). Once again, two additional adjustments to the tax-to-GDP ratio are made – first, SSCs are excluded, and second, voluntary contributions to government and compulsory contributions to the private sector are included. As mentioned previously, when no adjustments are made to the tax-to-GDP ratio, Chile's tax-to-GDP ratio is below the OECD average and has been for some time (in 2019, 20.7% compared to 33.8% respectively and in 1990 16.9% compared to 31.1% respectively), despite Chile's tax-to-GDP catch-up in recent decades[8]. Consequently, the gap between Chile and the OECD narrowed over the period by 1.1 percentage points (from 14.2pp in 1990 to 13.1pp in 2018).

Between 1990 and 2019, when compulsory contributions to the private sector are included in the tax-to-GDP ratio, Chile narrows the tax-to-GDP gap with the OECD average by 4.5 percentage points. Since not all countries had the data to make these adjustments in both years, the analysis is based on a smaller sample of countries. When VCs and CCs are included, Chile's tax-to-GDP is 26.9% in 2018 and 20.0% in 1990, compared to 35.1% in the OECD and 32.8% in 1990. Therefore, Chile's tax-to-GDP ratio narrowed the gap with the OECD by 4.5 percentage points (from a gap of 12.8 percentage points in 1990 to 8.2 percentage points in 2018). On this basis, Chile would have the 6th lowest tax-to-GDP ratio.

Between 1990 and 2019, when SSCs are excluded from the tax-to-GDP ratio, Chile narrowed the tax-to-GDP gap with the OECD average by 4.7 percentage points. When SSCs are excluded, Chile's tax-to-GDP is 19.6% in 2018 (15.4% in 1990), compared to 24.0% in the OECD (24.4% in 1990). Therefore, when SSCs are excluded, Chile's tax-to-GDP ratio grew much more quickly than the OECD (which in fact declined), resulting in Chile narrowing the absolute gap with the OECD average by 4.7 percentage points (from 9.0 percentage points in 1990 to 4.4 percentage points in 2018). On this basis, Chile would have the 6th lowest tax-to-GDP ratio.

Figure 3.4. When the tax-to-GDP ratio definition is adjusted to account for Chile's atypical tax structure, Chile remains among the lower tax-to-GDP OECD countries

Tax-to-GDP ratios, excluding SSCs and including voluntary contributions to government and compulsory contributions (CC) to the private sector, 1990 and 2018

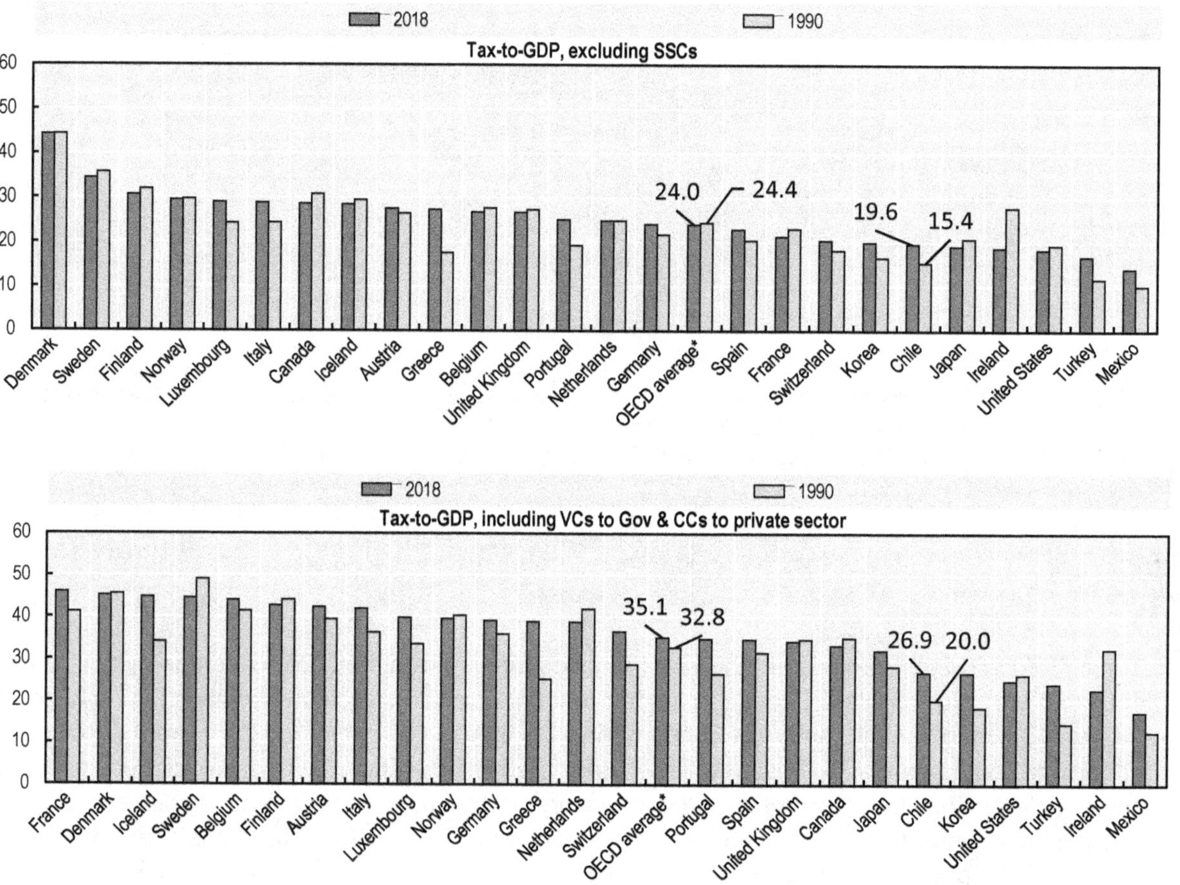

Note: Countries are only included if they had tax-to-GDP in 1990 and 2018 with SSCs, voluntary contributions to government and compulsory contributions to the private sector. For 1990 data are not available for Estonia, Poland, Slovenia, Slovak Republic, Hungary, Israel, and Czech Republic. Countries which joined the OECD after 1990 and for which data are not available in 1990 are not included. *The OECD average represents a simple weighted average of countries in which data are available in 1990 and 2018.
Source: OECD (2020), Revenue Statistics 2020, OECD Publishing, Paris, https://doi.org/10.1787/8625f8e5-en.

Broadly similar tax rates in Chile and the OECD point to low tax revenues driven by a narrow tax base, particularly in the case of PIT

Chile's CIT rate in 2020 is above the average CIT rate in the OECD, having increased over the past 20 years in contrast to a widespread decline in the OECD average rate. Table 3.2 provides a simple comparison of selected statutory tax rates in Chile and the OECD average in 2020 and 2000 (a more detailed comparison of tax rates goes beyond the scope of this research). Chile's combined CIT rate is

27% in 2020, which is somewhat higher than the OECD average rate of 23.5%. Chile's combined CIT rate has increased significantly since 2000 when it was 15%. By contrast, in the OECD generally there has been a steady and widespread decline in CIT rates over the past decade, although some countries have introduced or announced new tax increases over the past year. Overall, in the OECD, the average combined (central and sub-central) CIT rate has declined from 32.2% in 2000 to 23.5% in 2020.

Chile's VAT rate is similar to the average VAT rate in the OECD, having remained stable over the past 20 years similar to the OECD average rate. Chile's standard VAT rate is 19% in 2020, which is similar to the OECD average of 19.3%. The VAT rate has increased modestly from 2000 when it was 18%. In OECD countries, the VAT rate increased steadily from 18% in 2000. Raising standard VAT rates was a common strategy for countries seeking to achieve fiscal consolidation in the wake of the global financial crisis as increasing VAT rates provides immediate revenues without directly affecting competitiveness and has generally been found to be less detrimental to economic growth than raising direct taxes (Johansson et al., 2008[9]).

Despite a high top PIT rate, the tax burden on individuals is low in Chile driven by a narrow PIT base. Chile's top PIT rate is 40% in 2020 (based on the second category income tax rate), which is modestly lower than the OECD average rate of 42.8%. Chile's top PIT rate has declined modestly from 45% in 2000, similar to the trend of the OECD average rate. However, Chile's top PIT rate only applies at high levels of income and does not apply to the vast majority of individual taxpayers. Consequently, the low tax burden on individuals in Chile is not driven by the PIT rate (or the PIT rate threshold) but rather by the narrow PIT base and a high basic allowance. Low revenues from the PIT, including from taxes on capital income, are caused by other factors as well, including generous PIT expenditures. Notably, 76% of Chileans that file tax returns are in the exempt bracket (OECD, 2018[6]). As a result, the effective tax burden on individuals based on OECD *Taxing Wages* - measured by the total tax wedge for single persons earning the average wage - was only 7% in 2019 in Chile compared to 25.9% in the OECD average (note that this low effective tax burden on individuals in Chile reflects only a 7% contribution for health and does not take account of Chilean SSCs).

Similar tax rates in Chile and the OECD suggest that raising the relatively low levels of tax revenues in Chile might better be achieved through tax base (rather than tax rate) reform. Despite Chile's relatively low tax revenues (see Section 2.2), this simple tax rate comparison highlights that some of Chile's main tax rates in 2020 are similar to the OECD average. If Chile decides to raise additional tax revenues, the analysis provides suggestive evidence that there may be greater scope to do so through base broadening (e.g. limiting tax expenditures rather than tax rate increases and reducing tax evasion and avoidance) and rebalancing the tax mix (e.g. by increasing personal income tax revenues, including revenues from taxes on capital income).

Table 3.2. While tax rates in Chile are broadly similar to average rates in the OECD, the effective tax burden on individuals is low

% tax rates on individuals, companies and goods and services in Chile and the OECD, 2000 and 2020

		2020		2000	
Taxes on	**Measured by**	**Chile**	**OECD average**	**Chile**	**OECD average**
Individuals	Top PIT rate	40.0	42.8	45.0	45.4
Individuals	Tax wedge	7.0	25.9		
Companies	Combined CIT rate	27.0	23.5	15.0	32.2
Goods & Services	Standard VAT rate	19.0	19.3	18.0*	18.0

Note: *The standard VAT rate in Chile relates to the year 1995. Combined statutory CIT rates refer to central and sub-central statutory CIT rates. Chile's top PIT rate of 40% relates to the second category income tax. The tax wedge refers to single persons with no children at the average wage based on *OECD Taxing Wages*.
Source: OECD (2020), OECD Tax Database Statistics 2020, https://stats.oecd.org/Index.aspx?DataSetCode=TABLE_I1

4 Tax convergence

This chapter begins by considering the historical growth pattern of tax-to-GDP in OECD countries. The chapter then examines theoretical and empirical evidence for whether low tax-to-GDP countries catch-up with high tax-to-GDP countries over time (known as beta tax convergence) and whether Chile's tax structure has become more similar to the OECD average over time (known as sigma tax convergence).

A growing tax-to-GDP over time has been the historical norm across countries on average, but is far from guaranteed in individual countries

The tax-to-GDP ratio grew at an average annual rate of about two percentage points per decade in the OECD, based on historical data. Does the tax-to-GDP ratio grow over time and by how much? Forecasting future tax-to-GDP ratios is uncertain and challenging and there are many methods for producing economic forecasts. One such method is to estimate the future tax-to-GDP ratio path based on long-term historical average data. There are caveats to this method including that it does not take into account current economic conditions and its accuracy depends on the extent to which the future tax-to-GDP ratio is well-explained by the historical tax-to-GDP ratio. Notwithstanding these caveats, using 1965 as the base year, Figure 4.1 shows that the tax-to-GDP ratio increased on average in the OECD by 3.7, 7.9 and 9.7 percentage points cumulatively over 10, 20 and 30 years. The maximum tax-to-GDP ratio increase in any OECD country was 9.4 percentage points after ten years, 14.5 percentage points after 20 years and 17.4 percentage points after 30 years. Over the full period 1965 to 2019, the average annual tax-to-GDP increase was 0.21 percentage points or 2.1 percentage points in ten years. In a given year, the maximum tax-to-GDP increase was 5.1 percentage points and the minimum was decline of 5.6 percentage points. The top 10% of tax-to-GDP ratio increases was 1.4 percentage points.

While a rising tax-to-GDP ratio is the historical norm across OECD countries on average, it is far from guaranteed in individual countries. The tax-to-GDP ratio is not necessarily an indicator that converges in the same way as has been shown in the literature for GDP per capita. By definition, for a given level of tax revenues in a country, any increase in GDP will reduce the tax-to-GDP ratio. Ireland is a case in point. Even as Ireland's economy began to converge with the OECD and its GDP per capita grew, its tax-to-GDP ratio fell. Figure 4.1 also highlights that, in the first 35 years since 1965, the average tax-to-GDP ratio rose significantly but it remained broadly constant since then (with the exception of fluctuations during economic crises).

Figure 4.1. Tax-to-GDP ratios have tended to grow over time in the past

Mean, max and min cumulative growth rates in tax-to-GDP ratio in OECD countries over time (base year = 1965)

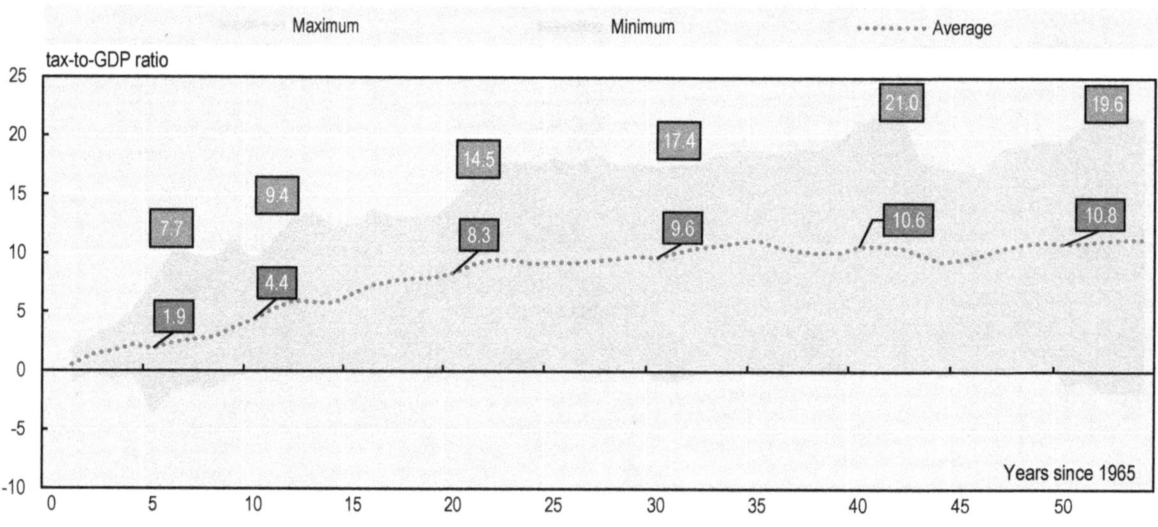

Note: Analysis conducted on the 23 OECD countries for which data is available between 1965 and 2019. Latest data for Australia and Japan is for 2018.
Source: OECD (2020), Revenue Statistics 2020, OECD Publishing, Paris, https://doi.org/10.1787/8625f8e5-en.

Evidence points to tax convergence among countries over time

Tax convergence is measured using the tax-to-GDP ratio in the research literature. How is convergence and tax convergence defined? In the field of economics, convergence generally refers to economic convergence, which can be defined as whether poor economies close the gap with rich economies over time (measured using GDP per capita). A vast literature exists on economic convergence. Neoclassical growth theory states that open economies with access to the same technology should converge to a common income level (Barro and Sala-i-Martin, 1992[10]) (Mankiw, Romer and Weil, 1992[11]). Fiscal convergence, a hotly researched topic in international tax, has been defined in the literature in different ways including in terms of tax convergence which is measured in terms of the tax-to-GDP ratio (Tibulca, 2015[12])[9]. For the purposes of the current research, this latter definition of tax convergence is used.

Tax convergence can be measured in different ways according to the research literature. The approaches used to measure economic convergence can also be applied to tax convergence. Two commonly adopted approaches to measure tax convergence are sigma (hereafter σ-convergence) and beta convergence (hereafter β-convergence)[10]. The meaning of the term convergence is somewhat different in each case, which is worth understanding. β-convergence refers to the speed of tax convergence (Baumol, 1986[13]). β-convergence has been the dominant method for about 25 years to test whether poorer countries tend to grow faster (Kant, 2019[5]). In a tax convergence context, it tells us whether low-tax countries catch-up (in terms of their tax-to-GDP ratio) with high-tax countries over time. β-convergence occurs in a group of countries when those with below-average tax-to-GDP ratios grow their tax-to-GDP ratios faster than those with above-average tax-to-GDP ratios over time. σ-convergence, on the other hand, occurs in a group of countries when there is a decline in the dispersion of the tax-to-GDP ratio over time. σ-convergence can be measured using a range of dispersion indicators including standard deviation, coefficient of variation (CV), the absolute deviation from the average, Gini coefficient and range measures. Of these indicators, CV is perhaps the most commonly adopted. β-convergence is a necessary but not a sufficient condition for σ-convergence because below-average economies must grow faster than above-average economies for there to be a decline in dispersion. σ-convergence provides a more accurate indication of convergence because it shows whether the dispersion of the entire distribution is declining.

Table 4.1. Two key measures of convergence are beta and sigma convergence

Convergence measure	Answers the question of	Stylized fact	Policy questions
Beta (β-convergence)	How fast are poorer economies catching-up with richer economies?	In a group of countries, those with below-average incomes grow faster than those with above-average incomes over time	Does tax convergence occur in a similar way to economic convergence?
Sigma (σ-convergence)	Are countries becoming more similar over time? Is a group of economies converging or diverging from its average?	There is a decline in dispersion over time	Do countries adopt policies so that they converge to the group over time? Do 'convergence clubs' exist?

Source: (OECD, 2018[3]) (Esteve, Sosvilla-Rivero and Tamarit, 2000[14]) (Tibulca, 2015[12]).

Evidence from the research literature generally points to tax convergence over time. Does the evidence from the research literature suggest that countries adopt policies that cause them to converge with the group average (tax-to-GDP ratio) over time? Table 4.2 provides evidence that the answer to this question is yes – tax convergence is often detected over time (as opposed to tax divergence). Table 4.2 also confirms that tax convergence is commonly measured using the measures of σ-convergence and β-convergence. However, the summary results provided in Table 4.2 should be interpreted with caution because of the different methodological approaches used in the studies. For example, there are differences in the tax convergence measures, time periods and countries and regions under examination.

Table 4.2. Some evidence points to tax convergence over time

Selected research on tax convergence

Research author	Convergence measures used	Period	Convergence identified (1)
Esteve et al. (2000)	Sigma, beta	1967 - 1994	Yes
Sosvilla et al. (2001)	Sigma (standard deviation), beta	1967 – 1995	Yes
Delgado (2006)	Sigma, beta and gamma	1965 – 2003	Yes
Gemmel and Kneller (2003)	Sigma (Gini coefficient)	1970 - 1995	
Tibulca (2015)	Sigma (coefficient of variation; Gini coefficient)	1965 - 2012	Yes
OECD (2018)	Sigma (d-index)	1995 - 2016	Yes
Delgado and Presno (2008)	Beta convergence	1965 - 2005	No
Chen et al. (2015)	Sigma and beta convergence	1980 - 2014	Yes

Note: (1) Refers to cases where any convergence was identified during any period as part of the research. The study by Chen et al. (2008) estimates corporate income tax convergence using corporate income tax rates and not tax-to-GDP ratios.
Source: Table adapted from (Tibulca, 2015[12]) (OECD, 2018[3]).

Despite the evidence for tax convergence across countries, it is not guaranteed for individual countries without the right conditions in place. Some of the economic convergence literature argues that economic convergence is conditional and occurs only when country specific conditions are in place including specific policies, institutional arrangements and external shocks. This suggests that the policies that successful countries have used are hard to emulate and that transplanting experience from one country to another is difficult and 'convergence is anything but automatic' (Rodrik, 2011[15]). A similar line of reasoning might apply to tax convergence whereby certain country-specific policies and institutional arrangements may first need to be in place for tax-to-GDP ratios to grow over time. However, it important to note that GDP per capita and tax-to-GDP ratios are very different measures. –There seem to be evidence that the tax-to-GDP ratio cannot continue to increase beyond some point when it begins to become damaging to economic activity and this is evidenced in the historical upper bound tax-to-GDP ratio of about 50% in OECD countries (see Figure 2.3).

Empirical evidence supports the notion that low tax-to-GDP OECD countries catch-up over time (beta convergence)

Beta tax convergence can be empirically confirmed through correlation and econometric analysis. This section explores the evidence for whether lower tax-to-GDP countries like Chile tend to catch-up with higher tax-to-GDP on average over time (i.e. beta-convergence), based on OECD countries in recent decades. From an empirical perspective, tax β-convergence can be confirmed by showing a tendency for countries with lower tax-to-GDP ratios to increase their tax-to-GDP ratios faster than countries with higher tax-to-GDP ratios over time. Using correlational analysis, this can be confirmed by a negative slope in a two-way scatterplot. Using econometric analysis, this can be confirmed by a statistically significant negative sign of the estimated coefficient.

Correlation analysis on OECD historical data confirm that tax-to-GDP convergence occurs among OECD countries over time. Figure 4.2 shows that a higher starting tax-to-GDP ratio is indeed associated with smaller subsequent growth in the tax-to-GDP ratio among OECD countries over time, based on OECD revenue statistics data. Tax-to-GDP convergence is confirmed by the observed negative downward sloping line. Conversely, it follows that countries with lower tax-to-GDP ratios grow their tax-to-GDP ratios faster on average than countries with larger tax-to-GDP ratios. Figure 4.2 also shows that the tax-to-GDP convergence has been stronger over the past half-century (1965 – 2019) than in the more recent past quarter-century (1995 – 2019). This is observed in the steeper downward negative correlation between starting tax-to-GDP and subsequent growth in tax-to-GDP during this period and the higher average subsequent growth in tax-to-GDP.

Figure 4.2. There is evidence of β-convergence in OECD countries over the past half century

Log of tax-to-GDP and the log difference in tax-to-GDP ratio, 1995 – 2019 and 1965 – 2019

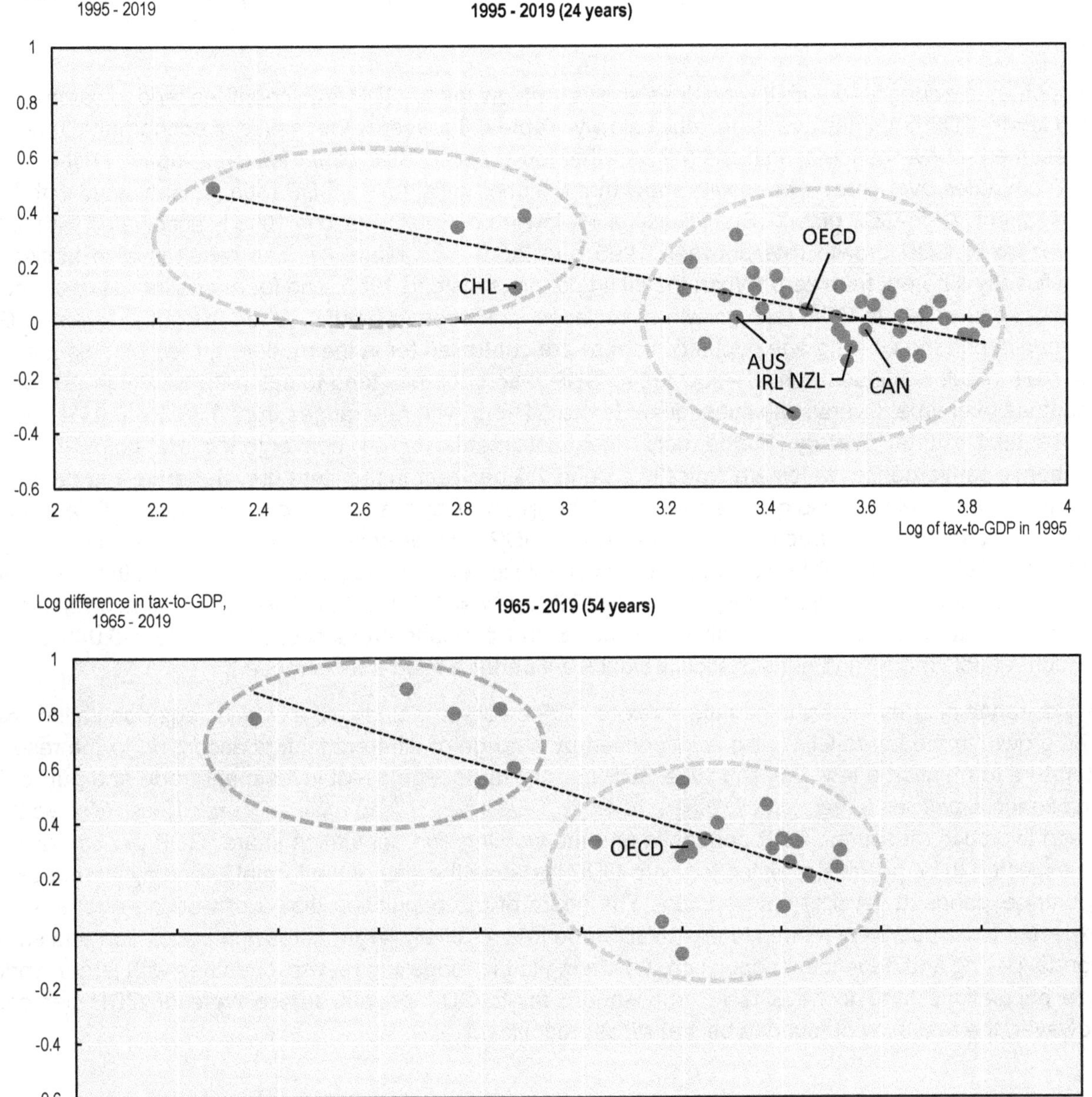

Note: Data for Australia and Japan is 2018. Natural logs are used. The set of OECD countries for which data is available in both years in 1965 and 2019 is smaller (i.e. in the bottom graph).
Source: OECD (2020), Revenue Statistics 2020, OECD Publishing, Paris, https://doi.org/10.1787/8625f8e5-en.

An econometric equation can be formulated to test β-convergence. To test β-convergence econometrically, a log-log Ordinary Least Squares (OLS) regression model is employed using robust standard errors (to account for heteroscedasticity[11]). The data used are country-level OECD revenue statistics for the two periods 1965 to 2019 and 1995 to 2019 respectively. The specification is set out in equation (1) below, where ΔY is the change in the tax-to-GDP over the period, Y_{it-1} is tax-to-GDP in the starting year and Z_{it-1} is a set of explanatory variables in the starting year including GDP per capita and the working age population. Beta-convergence can be confirmed by a statistically significant negative sign of $\beta 1$.

$$\Delta(\log) Y_{it} = a + \beta_1 (\log) Y_{it-1} + \beta_2 Z_{it-1} + U_{it} \qquad (1)$$

Econometric evidence for OECD countries shows that low tax-to-GDP ratio countries tend to catch-up with high tax-to-GDP countries over time, albeit slowly. Table 4.3 presents the results of econometric modelling to test the β-convergence hypothesis (i.e. whether lower tax-to-GDP countries catch-up with richer tax-to-GDP countries over time). The results show that a higher initial tax-to-GDP ratio is associated with lower subsequent tax-to-GDP growth. Specifically, a 1% lower tax-to-GDP ratio in 1995 is associated with 0.36% higher tax-to-GDP growth rate between 1995 and 2019 (see Model 1). The result is also statistically significantly different from zero. When the initial period is instead 1965, and for a smaller set of countries, the subsequent tax-to-GDP ratio growth association increases to 0.60%. When the initial levels of GDP per capita and the working age population share are controlled for in the modelling (see Models 2 and 3), the main result continues to hold – low tax-to-GDP ratio countries tend to catch-up with high tax-to-GDP countries over time. Overall, the subsequent tax-to-GDP growth rate ranges from 0.36% – 0.44% over the subsequent quarter century. Furthermore, these estimates for tax convergence are below those for economic convergence, which are typically around 2% per year in the literature. Separately, a panel data econometric model was also explored as part of this analysis by restructuring the same OECD tax-to-GDP data into a longitudinal structure where the tax-to-GDP ratio is observed in 36 countries in each year between 1995 and 2019. When the dependent variable is set as the log of tax-to-GDP and the explanatory variable is the five-year lag of the log of tax-to-GDP, the results show that the β-convergence remains but the magnitude is substantially smaller than under the previous cross-sectional model (-0.045 under a random effects model and not statistically significant under a fixed effects model).

A wide range of other factors contribute to tax-to-GDP catch-up including the working age population share. The growth in the tax-to-GDP ratio is influenced by a range of different factors according to the research literature to mention a few, these include GDP per capita, foreign direct investment trade and public debt and financial policies (Gupta, 2007, Bird et al, 2008, Teera and Hudson, 2004, Tanzi, 1988). Models 2 and 3 add two such measures, GDP per capita and the working age population share. GDP per capita would be expected to be positively related to tax-to-GDP because the size of the formal economy increases as a country expands its level of development. The share of the population that is of working age is also be expected to be positively related to tax-to-GDP due to a relatively larger taxpaying population and smaller non-taxpaying and dependent population. According to the modelling results, countries with larger working age populations tend to have faster subsequent tax-to-GDP growth. In the case of GDP per capita however, the result is not found to be statistically significant.

Table 4.3. Econometric evidence supports the hypothesis that low tax-to-GDP OECD countries tend to catch-up over time

Econometric evidence for the conditional β-convergence hypothesis, various OECD data, 1995 – 2019

	Dependent variable: log difference of tax-to-GDP ratio				
	1995 – 2019			1965 - 2019	
	OLS (1)	OLS (2)	OLS (3)	OLS (4)	OLS (5)
Log of tax-to-GDP in 1995	-0.36*** (-8.59)	-0.39*** (-8.56)	-0.44*** (-8.00)	-0.60*** (-6.87)	-0.60*** (-5.52)
Log of GDP per capita in 1995		0.47 (1.65)	0.40 (1.31)		0.002 (0.02)
Log of working age pop 1995			1.16** (2.39)		
R-squared	0.50	0.52	0.58	0.55	0.55
No. observations	36	36	36	24	24

Note: ***p<0.01, **p<0.05 *p<0.10. Robust t-statistics in brackets. Models 1 through 3 are based on 36 countries between 1995 and 2019. Models 4 and 5 are based on a smaller set of 25 countries between 1965 and 2019.
Source: OECD (2020), Revenue Statistics 2020, OECD Publishing, Paris, https://doi.org/10.1787/8625f8e5-en.

Chile's tax mix has converged slowly with the OECD average tax mix, but more slowly than individual countries (sigma convergence)

The extent to which OECD country tax structures have converged can be measured using the D-index. Are tax structures in OECD countries converging or diverging (i.e. becoming more or less similar)? This question can be addressed using a number of sigma-convergence type measures which examine the similarity of tax structures across countries. One method is the D-index (Delgado, 2013[16]), which provides an indicator of the difference between a country's tax structure from a group average like the OECD. The D-index is calculated as the absolute difference in each tax category share for a given country from the OECD share. The tax categories are then summed for each country. With regard to interpretation, a value of zero would indicate that the country's tax structure is the same as the OECD average structure. For all OECD countries between 1965 and 2019, the D-index averaged 44, with a maximum value of 112 and a minimum of 10. In the OECD, it was 50 in 1965 and 59 in 2019 (OECD, 2018[3]).

The D-index suggests that the OECD may be a tax 'convergence club', which implies that lower tax-to-GDP countries like Chile may tend to converge with the OECD average over time. Do countries adopt polices so that they converge to the average of the group or does tax policy remain largely nationally focused? Some strands of the economic convergence literature have examined the notion of 'convergence clubs' where poorer countries (measured in terms of GDP per capita) that are part of a group of countries (such as the OECD) tend to converge to the group average GDP per capita over time (Quah, 1995[17]). To the extent that the OECD is a 'convergence club' where members share knowledge and best practice, observing no convergence at all would be a concern. The D-index provides one way of empirically testing whether the OECD could be a tax 'convergence club'. Figure 4.3 shows that the tax structure of individual OECD countries have become more similar to each other over the past half century since 1965 as measured by the D-index (which declined by 36% between 1965 and 2018). This result provides suggestive evidence that the OECD may be a tax 'convergence club'. The causes underlying this tax convergence are varied and complex and go beyond the scope of this paper, however, one partial explanation could be that OECD countries tend to adopt policies that cause their tax-to-GDP ratio to converge to the average of the group. If this result were to hold for the future, it would imply that lower tax-to-GDP ratio countries such as Chile will tend to rise and converge with the OECD average tax structure over time

Chile has converged with the average OECD tax structure, but more slowly than other OECD countries. Figure 4.3 shows that, since 1995, Chile and the selected OECD countries have slowly converged with the OECD average tax structure (Chile's and the OECD average D-index declined by 12% and 14% respectively between 1995 and 2018). However, Chile has converged more slowly than the individual OECD countries have with the OECD average (i.e. become more similar to each other in terms of their tax structure).

Figure 4.3. Chile's tax mix has converged slowly with the OECD average tax mix, but more slowly than individual OECD countries

D-index in Chile, selected countries and the OECD, 1965 - 2018

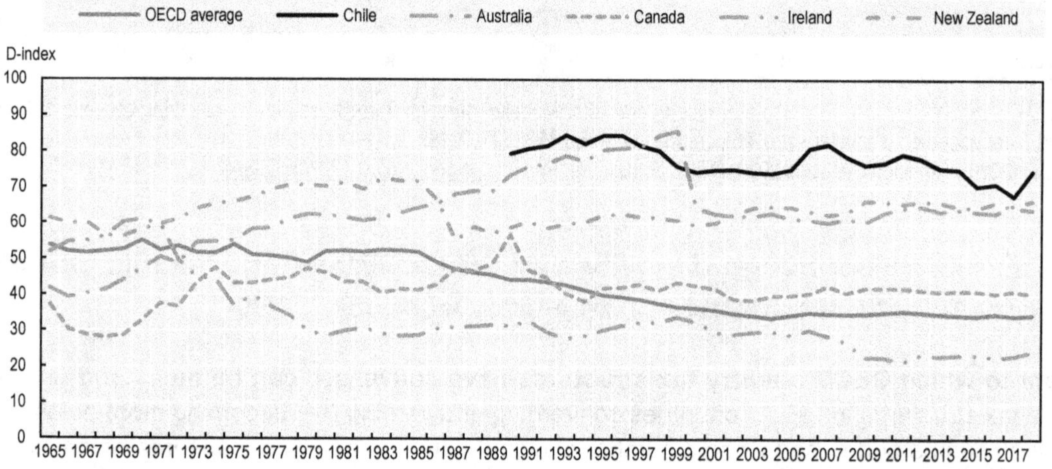

Note: The D-index refers to the sum of the absolute difference in tax structures in countries compared to the OECD average in a given year. The OECD average is calculated as the mean average of the sum of the absolute differences in all OECD countries, which provides an indicator of the extent to which tax structures are different or similar across countries in the OECD.
Source: OECD (2020), Revenue Statistics 2020, OECD Publishing, Paris, https://doi.org/10.1787/8625f8e5-en.

Chile's tax structure differs significantly from the OECD average

Among OECD countries, Chile's tax structure is one of the most divergent from the OECD average. Is Chile's tax structure similar to the OECD average? Figure 4.4 shows the sum of absolute differences in tax structure for OECD countries in 2018 and 1995. Countries with the greatest tax structure difference from the OECD, as measured by the highest D-index, include those without SSCs (Australia, Denmark, New Zealand), without VAT (United States) and with relatively high VAT and low SSCs and PIT (Chile). Among OECD countries, Chile's tax structure is one of the most divergent from the OECD average in 2018, although the absolute difference between Chile and the OECD has fallen modestly since 1995.

Figure 4.4. Chile's tax structure is least similar to the OECD average

D-index* in Chile and OECD countries, 2018 and 1995

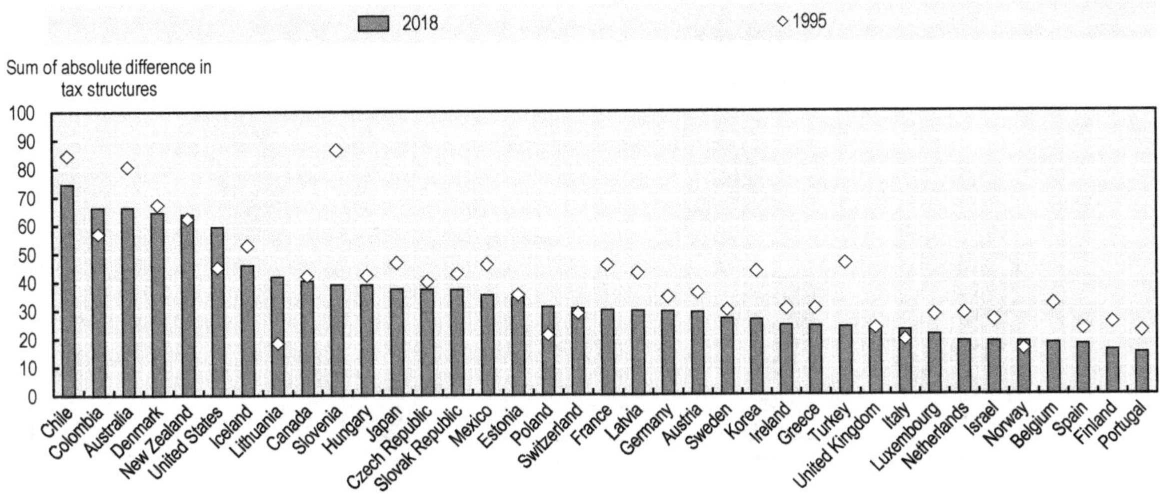

Note: *The D-index refers to the sum of the absolute difference in tax structures in countries compared to the OECD average in a given year. The tax categories are then summed for each country. With regard to interpretation, a value of 0 would indicate that the country's tax structure is the same as the OECD average structure. For all OECD countries between 1965 and 2019, the D-index averaged 44, with a maximum value of 112 and a minimum of 10. In the OECD, it was 50 in 1965 and 59 in 2019

Source: OECD (2020), Revenue Statistics 2020, OECD Publishing, Paris, https://doi.org/10.1787/8625f8e5-en.

When compulsory contributions to the private sector are included, Chile's tax structure moves closer to the OECD average but remains among the least similar the OECD average tax structure. Is Chile's tax structure similar the OECD average when contributions to the private sector are accounted for? Figure 4.5 shows an adjusted D-index calculation which includes voluntary contributions to government and compulsory contributions to the private sector. These contributions are added to SSCs and payroll taxes, which are grouped together in the D-index calculation for each country. A number of further caveats are worth noting including that data on compulsory private contributions are not available for all countries in 1990 and 2018 and that the OECD average is based on a changing number of countries over time (for more detailed methodological notes, see notes in Figure 4.5). Overall, Chile's unadjusted D-index is 79.5 in 1990 and 74.5 in 2018 while its adjusted index is 69.8 in 1990 and 59.9 in 2018. As a result, when compulsory contributions to the private sector are included as part of SSCs (i.e. the adjusted D-index) Chile's tax structure looks more similar to the OECD average tax structure than when unadjusted (note that the D-index has also changed for other OECD countries as a result of the adjustment). However, even after the D-index is adjusted, Chile's remains among the most dissimilar OECD countries in terms of its tax structure to the OECD average.

Figure 4.5. Chile's tax structure moves closer to the OECD average structure when the D-index is adjusted to include compulsory contributions to the private sector

Adjusted country D-index* relative to the OECD average, Chile and selected countries, in 1990 and 2018

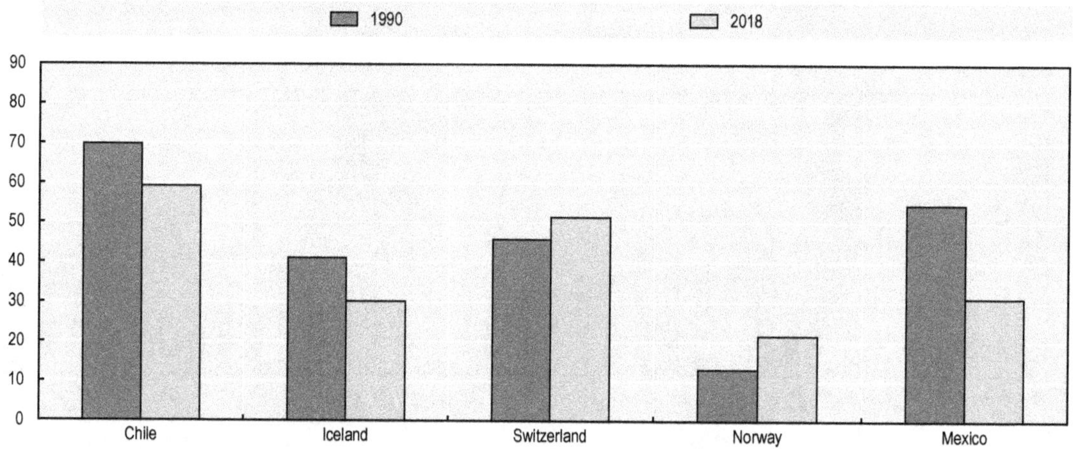

Note: The D-index refers to the sum of the absolute difference in tax structures in countries compared to the OECD average in a given year. *The adjusted D-index has been recalculated by adding voluntary contributions to government and compulsory contributions to the private sector to SSCs and payroll taxes (which are grouped together for the purposes of the D-index analysis) for all countries in 1990 and 2018. There are 25 countries were voluntary contributions to government and compulsory payments to the private sector are available in 1990 and 2018. Note that the addition of these contributions changes SSCs for these 25 countries but also for the OECD average and therefore the calculation of the absolute difference between countries and the OECD average. Consequently, the adjusted D-index calculations will be different than the unadjusted D-index calculations for all countries.
Source: OECD (2020), Revenue Statistics 2020, OECD Publishing, Paris, https://doi.org/10.1787/8625f8e5-en.

Chile's tax structure gap with the OECD is driven by VAT and PIT, when contributions to the private sector are included in SSCs

When compulsory contributions to the private sector and voluntary contributions to government are added to SSCs in all countries, the gap between Chile's tax structure and the OECD average is driven by VAT and PIT. Which taxes drive the tax structure gap between Chile and the OECD average? The top chart in Figure 4.6 shows the absolute differences in tax structure between Chile and the OECD in 1990 and 2018. The largest differences are observed for SSCs (plus payroll), VAT, PIT and CIT. The bottom chart in Figure 4.6 shows the difference in Chile's tax structure when the above adjusted D-index methodology is applied (i.e. voluntary contributions to government and compulsory contributions to the private sector are added to SSCs and payroll taxes for all countries). On this basis, SSCs and payroll taxes in Chile are now similar to the OECD average (unlike in the case of the previous unadjusted D-index) and the gap between Chile's tax structure and the OECD average is primarily driven by VAT and PIT revenues.

Figure 4.6. The difference in Chile's tax structure compared to the OECD average is driven primarily by the gap in VAT and PIT

Absolute difference in tax structure between Chile and the OECD average, unadjusted and adjusted for compulsory payments to the private sector, 1990 and 2018

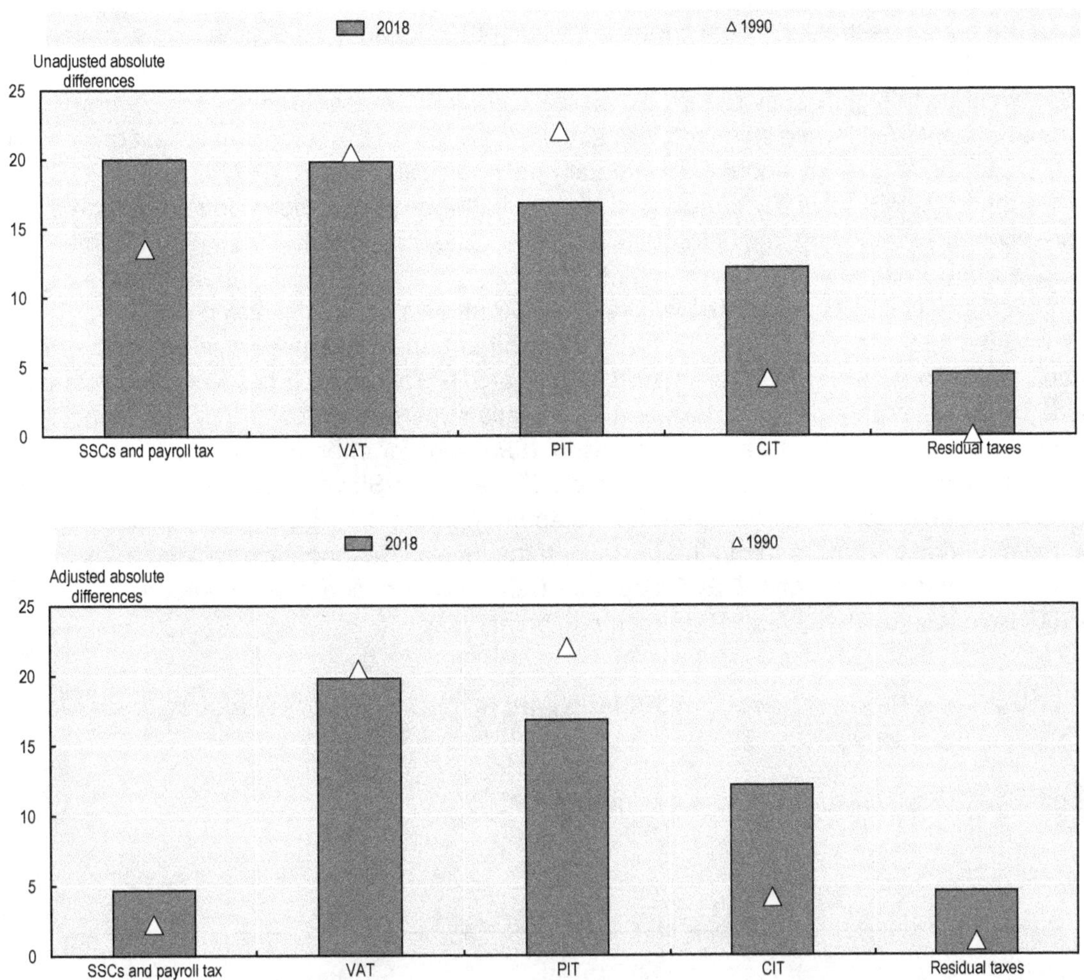

Note: Absolute differences refer to a non-negative differences between the country and the OECD average structure.
Source: OECD (2020), Revenue Statistics 2020, OECD Publishing, Paris, https://doi.org/10.1787/8625f8e5-en.

Some evidence suggests that lower income countries have the potential for faster subsequent tax-to-GDP growth

Some evidence points to tax-to-GDP ratios growing faster in countries that have lower starting income levels, but only up to a point. A related but different question to tax convergence is whether poorer countries (measured by lower GDP per capita) tend to experience greater tax-to-GDP ratio growth than richer countries over time. Figure 4.7 shows tax-to-GDP growth in Chile and in the OECD between 1995 and 2019 based on GDP per capita quartiles in 1995. The analysis provides some evidence that tax-to-GDP ratios grow faster on average for countries with lower starting levels of GDP per capita, but only up to a point. Countries that were in the bottom quartile of the OECD in GDP per capita in 1995 had faster subsequent tax-to-GDP growth than richer countries in the second and third GDP per capita quartiles.

However, countries who were in the top quartile of GDP per capita in 1995 had the fastest tax-to-GDP growth over the period. Chile, which was in the bottom quartile of GDP per capita countries in 1995 (with a GDP per capita of USD 12 253), had a faster subsequent tax-to-GDP growth than the average in any quartile.

However, some countries with similar income levels have followed opposite paths tax-to-GDP trajectories. The association between GDP per capita and subsequent growth in the tax-to-GDP ratio is not particularly strong. Part of the reason is that individual countries, with both low and high income levels, have followed divergent tax-to-GDP paths. For example, Ireland, which had a relatively high GDP per capita in 1995 (USD 31 404), went on to significantly reduce its tax-to-GDP by 9.1 percentage points between 1995 and 2019. The reduced tax-to-GDP ratio in Ireland was substantially driven by exceptionally fast growth in GDP - Ireland's GDP per capita grew by about 7.0% annually between 1995 and 2019, compared to 1.8% in the OECD. A wide range factors have been proposed to explain the economic boom in Ireland (the so-called 'Celtic Tiger' economy) including the introduction of the Single European Market, FDI inflows from the United States into Ireland and a low corporate tax rate (Barry, 2003[18]). Ireland also provides an example of measurement issues associated with tax-to-GDP ratios, particularly how a single indicator such as GDP can mislead analysis (Honohan, 2021[19]). On the other hand, Luxembourg, which had a very high GDP per capita in 1995 (USD 71,920), increased its tax-to-GDP ratio by 4.5 percentage points over the same period. Similar divergent paths in the tax-to-GDP ratio occurred for lower income countries which were in the first quartile of GDP per capita countries in 1995, with for example Mexico increasing its tax-to-GDP by 6.4 percentage points between 1995 and 2019 and the Slovak Republic reducing its tax-to-GDP ratio by 4.8 percentage points. Furthermore, as seen in Figure 4.7, tax-to-GDP ratios in the OECD on average have tended to grow faster in the past when the levels of economic development were lower. For example, 10, 20 and 30 years after OECD countries had similar economic development levels to Chile, the tax-to-GDP ratio rose by 3.1, 2.5 and 0 percentage points respectively.

Figure 4.7. Countries with lower starting GDP per capita tended to have faster subsequent tax-to-GDP, but this was not always the case

Tax-to-GDP growth 1995 to 2019, by GDP per capita quartile in 1995

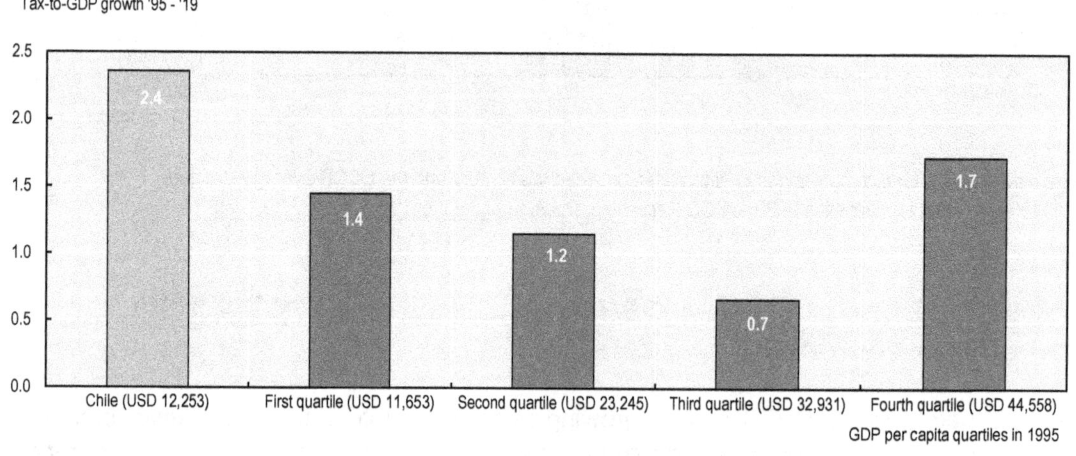

Note: Analysis based on 36 OECD countries between 1995 and 2019 divided into 4 quartiles based on GDP per capita levels in 1995 with 9 countries in each quartile. Australia and Canada tax-to-GDP data are for the year 2018. For comparability, the data are converted to a common currency, US dollars, using purchasing power parities (PPP). PPPs are currency converters that control for differences in the price levels between countries, making it possible to compare absolute values across countries.
Source: OECD (2020), Revenue Statistics 2020, OECD Publishing, Paris, https://doi.org/10.1787/8625f8e5-en and OECD Compendium of Productivity Indicators 2019, OECD Publishing, Paris, https://doi.org/10.1787/b2774f97-en

5 A tax-to-GDP ratio path for the future

This chapter begins by comparing Chile's tax-to-GDP ratio with countries when they had similar levels of economic development. It then projects a possible tax-to-GDP path for Chile over the coming decade if it were to follow the path of countries from when they had a similar level of economic development. However, the COVID-19 pandemic will make a rising tax-to-GDP ratio in the future in Chile much more challenging. Once the recovery is firmly in place, there is scope for Chile to re-examine its low tax level and rebalance its tax structure. The chapter also briefly highlights how some of the favourable demographics in Chile which helped to facilitate a low tax-to-GDP ratio are changing.

Chile's tax-to-GDP is low when compared with countries when they were at a similar level of economic development to Chile

Chile's tax-to-GDP ratio is similar to Australia when Australia had a similar level of GDP per capita to Chile's current level. In 2019[12], Chile had GDP per capita of USD 23 151 and a tax-to-GDP ratio of 20.7% in 2019. Table 5.1 shows that Australia, Canada, Ireland and New Zealand had the same GDP per capita as Chile's 2019 level in 1973, 1972, 1989 and 1975 respectively. Therefore, when Australia, Canada, Ireland and New Zealand had a similar level of economic development to Chile's[13], they had tax-to-GDP ratios of 22.5%, 29.9%, 32.5% and 30.0%. Chile's tax-to-GDP ratio is similar to Australia when Australia had a similar level of economic development. When the OECD average GDP per capita was similar to Chile's in 1978, the OECD average tax-to-GDP ratio was 31.1%.

Table 5.1. Chile's tax-to-GDP ratio is somewhat similar to Australia when Australia had a similar level of GDP per capita

Tax-to-GDP ratios of selected OECD countries, in the year in which they had the closest GDP per capita closest to Chile's in 2019 (Chile's tax-to-GDP ratio in 2019 = 20.7%)

	Year in which GDP per capita was the same as Chile's 2019 GDP per capita	Tax-to-GDP ratio in that year (t)	Tax-to-GDP ratio in that year, when SSCs are excluded (t)	Tax-to-GDP 10 years later (t + 10)	Tax-to-GDP 10 year change (in percentage points)
Australia	1973	22.5	22.5	26.1	3.6
Canada	1972	29.9	27.2	32.3	2.4
Ireland	1989	32.5	27.8	30.9	-1.6
New Zealand	1975	30.0	30.0	31.2	1.2
OECD average*	1978	31.1	23.0	34.3	3.1

Note: *Relates to 30 selected OECD countries for which data are available.
Source: OECD (2020), Revenue Statistics 2020, OECD Publishing, Paris, https://doi.org/10.1787/8625f8e5-en and OECD Compendium of Productivity Indicators 2019, OECD Publishing, Paris, https://doi.org/10.1787/b2774f97-en

Chile's tax-to-GDP ratio is low compared with OECD countries generally when they had similar GDP per capita to Chile's current level. Figure 5.1 shows the tax-to-GDP ratio for all OECD countries in the year in which they had the closest GDP per capita to Chile's 2019 GDP per capita level. The year in question for each country is shown in brackets in the graph. The analysis confirms that Chile's tax-to-GDP ratio is very low when compared with OECD countries when they had a similar level of economic development to Chile. Figure 5.1 also shows OECD countries when they had similar levels of economic development to Chile and SSCs are excluded from the tax-to-GDP ratio. On this basis, the tax-to-GDP ratio average across the OECD countries shown is 22.7% and ranges from 13.7% to 30.3%. This suggests that when SSCs are excluded Chile's tax-to-GDP ratio is only modestly below OECD countries when they had similar levels of economic development to Chile.

Figure 5.1. Chile's tax-to-GDP ratio is low compared with OECD countries when they had similar GDP per capita to Chile's current level

Tax-to-GDP ratios of OECD countries, in the year in which they had the closest GDP per capita closest to Chile's in 2019

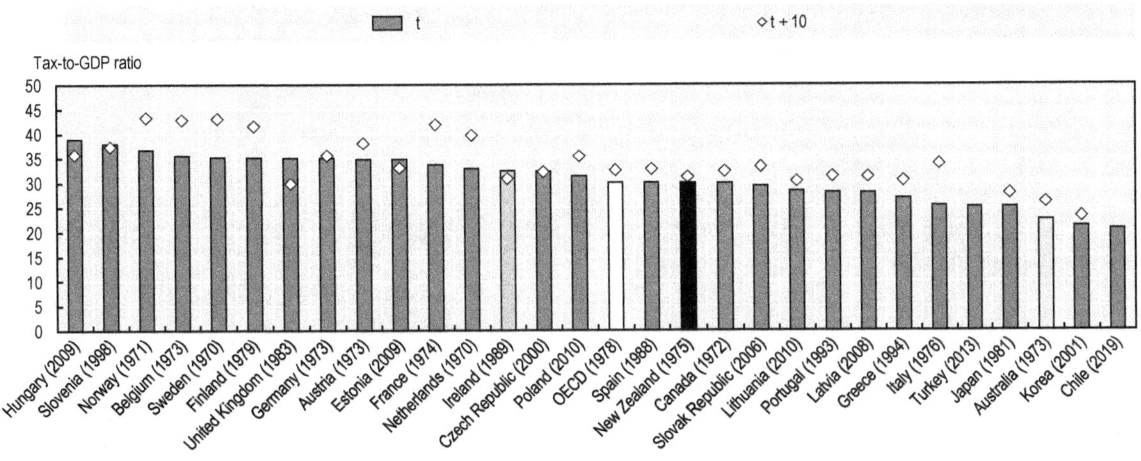

Note: The figure includes 28 OECD countries which had a similar GDP per capita (in PPP) to Chile's 2019 GDP per capita and which had tax-to-GDP data that was available in that year. t refers to the year in which the country had the closest GDP per capita to Chile's GDP per capita of USD 23,151 in 2019. t + 10 refers to the countries tax-to-GDP ratio ten years later. Poland and Lithuania do not have data ten years later so data 9 years later is used. Turkey does not have data ten years later (since the year in which had the same GDP per capita as Chile is 2013).
Source: OECD (2020), Revenue Statistics 2020, OECD Publishing, Paris, https://doi.org/10.1787/8625f8e5-en and OECD Compendium of Productivity Indicators 2019, OECD Publishing, Paris, https://doi.org/10.1787/b2774f97-en

A decade after OECD countries had similar incomes to Chile, the tax-to-GDP ratio had risen by three percentage points

Ten years after OECD countries had a similar level of economic development to Chile, the tax-to-GDP ratio had increased by three percentage points. Tax-to-GDP ratios have tended to rise in OECD countries on average over time from when they had similar levels of economic development to that in Chile currently. However, there is significant variation by country; individual country tax-to-GDP ratios can go up or down and for sustained periods. Ten years after OECD countries had similar economic development levels to Chile, tax-to-GDP rose by about 3pp on average. In Australia, it grew by 3.6pp but declined by 1.6pp in Ireland. According to the analysis, ten years after the year that Australia, Canada, Ireland and New Zealand had a similar level of economic development to Chile's current level, their tax-to-GDP ratios had changed to 26.1% (+3.6 percentage points), 32.3% (+2.4 percentage points), 30.9% (-1.6 percentage points) and 31.2% (+1.2 percentage points) respectively. Ten years after the OECD average had a similar level of economic development to Chile's current level, the OECD average tax-to-GDP ratio increased to 34.3%, which represents a change of 3.1 percentage points or 0.31 percentage points annually. Twenty years later, the OECD average tax-to-GDP ratio continued to increase, albeit more slowly to 36.7%, which represents an increase of 2.4 percentage points or 0.24 percentage points annually. The average tax-to-GDP growth for the four comparison countries is 1.4 percentage points over ten years or 0.14 percentage points a year.

Tax-to-GDP ratios tend to rise over time on average from lower levels of economic development, but they can also fluctuate up and down in individual countries for sustained periods. Figure 5.2 extends the analysis in Figure 5.1 to show yearly developments in the tax-to-GDP ratio in the OECD starting from the year in which they had the closest GDP per capita to Chile's 2019 level. The grey shaded area shows the range of the maximum and minimum tax-to-GDP level in a given country in each year. The analysis shows that, over a long-term 30 year time horizon, and for a group of advanced OECD countries, the average tax-to-GDP ratio has tended to rise from the time it had a level of economic development similar to Chile's level. After 10, 20 and 30 years, it had changed from 31.1% to 34.3% to 36.7% to 36.7% respectively. Note that in the last ten year period, the average tax-to-GDP ratio remained at the same level. However, the analysis also demonstrates that the tax-to-GDP level in individual countries can fluctuate downwards as well upwards and for sustained periods of time.

Figure 5.2. Tax-to-GDP ratios in individual countries can fluctuate down as well up and for sustained periods

Developments in tax-to-GDP ratios of OECD countries, starting from the year in which they had the closest GDP per capita closest to Chile's in 2019

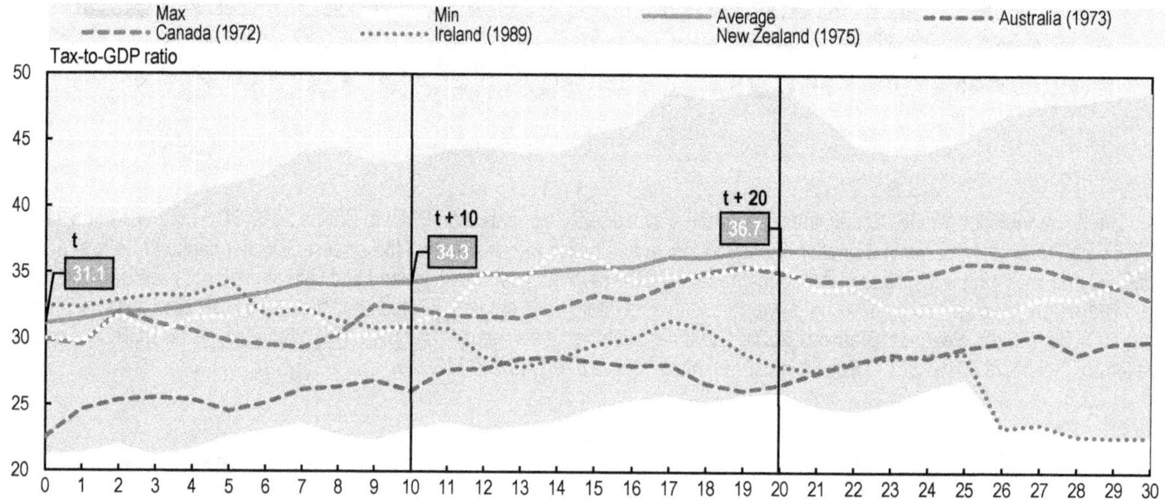

Note: The average refers to 28 OECD countries which had a similar GDP per capita in PPP to Chile's 2019 GDP per capita and which had tax-to-GDP data that was available in that year.
Source: OECD (2020), Revenue Statistics 2020, OECD Publishing, Paris, https://doi.org/10.1787/8625f8e5-en and OECD Compendium of Productivity Indicators 2019, OECD Publishing, Paris, https://doi.org/10.1787/b2774f97-en

While Chile's tax-to-GDP ratio path may have been set to rise, the COVID-19 pandemic and subsequent economic conditions have raised new challenges

There are many challenges to forecasting tax-to-GDP ratios, not least given the current environment. Forecasting tax-to-GDP ratios is uncertain and challenging and this is particularly true in the context of the impact of the COVID-19 pandemic and the prevailing economic conditions in the subsequent period. Beyond the immediate impact of COVID-19 and a strong bounce-back, the global economy is now facing elevated levels of inflation, tighter financial conditions and the impacts of the general withdrawal of extraordinary fiscal measures following the COVID-19 pandemic. There are many available methods to forecasting with differing advantages and limitations including using macroeconomic projections and historical statistical extrapolations. Under the latter approach, the future tax-to-GDP ratio path can be based on average long-term historical data. This approach comes with caveats including that it does not take into account current economic conditions and it assumes long-term historical trends will be representative of the future. Historical statistical extrapolations also do not take into account the role of tax buoyancy - whether GDP increases may cause higher tax revenues (for a discussion, see Section 1). Notwithstanding these caveats, Figure 5.3 provides an indication of possible paths based a historical statistical extrapolation using data for the year 2019 before the COVID-19 pandemic.

If Chile followed a similar path to the OECD average from when it had a similar level of economic development to Chile, Chile's tax-to-GDP could rise by 2029, but the COVID-19 pandemic has made this outcome more challenging. Notwithstanding these caveats, Figure 5.3 applies the tax-to-GDP trajectories in OECD countries from when they had similar GDP per capita to Chile in order to project a range of potential tax-to-GDP ratio outcomes for Chile over the next decade. If Chile were to follow a similar path to the average of OECD countries (when they had a similar level of economic development to Chile's current level), Chile's tax-to-GDP ratio in 2029 could reach 22.9%. However, a wide range of outcomes are possible ranging from 19.7% to 23.6% (shown in the shaded area) based on the historical trajectories of OECD countries as demonstrated by the fastest and slowest tax-to-GDP growth countries over the subsequent 10 year period. Importantly, the COVID-19 pandemic will make reaching the tax-to-GDP ratios presented in Chile much more uncertain.

Figure 5.3. If Chile's tax-to-GDP ratio were to follow various historical average trends, the tax-to-GDP ratio could rise by 2029

Chile's tax-to-GDP ratio in 2029, if it were to follow various paths

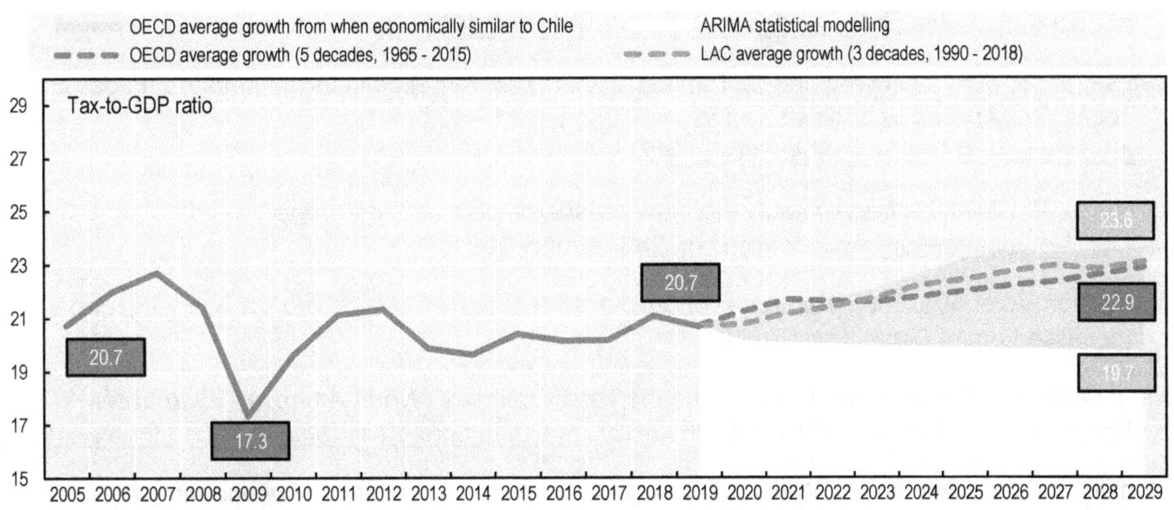

Note: (1) OECD average growth rate when economically similar to Chile relates to a set of 27 countries for which GDP per capita data can be matched and where tax-to-GDP data are available (ISR, ISL and TUR are not included). Fastest and slowest tax-to-GDP growth countries are selected after 10 years from the year in which GDP per capita was the same as Chile's 2019 GDP per capita. The OECD average growth from when countries were economically similar to Chile predicts a tax-to-GDP ratio of 23.6% in 2029 (2) OECD average growth is based on the average annual growth rate of OECD countries in the past five decades (from 1965 to 2015). (3) The LAC average growth rate is based on the average annual growth rate of LAC countries in the past three decades (from 1995 to 2018). (4) ARIMA modelling is based on Chile's historical tax-to-GDP path over 3 decades (between 1990 and 2019). The ARIMA modelling predicts a tax-to-GDP ratio of 19.7% in 2029.
Source: OECD (2020), Revenue Statistics 2020, OECD Publishing, Paris, https://doi.org/10.1787/8625f8e5-en

References

Barro, J. and X. Sala-i-Martin (1992), "Convergence", https://doi.org/10.1086/261816. [10]

Barry, F. (2003), "Tax Policy, FDI and the Irish Economic Boom of the 1990s", *Economic Analysis and Policy*, Vol. 33/2, pp. 221-236, https://doi.org/10.1016/S0313-5926(03)50018-2. [18]

Baumol, W. (1986), "American Economic Association Productivity Growth, Convergence, and Welfare: What the Long-Run Data Show", pp. 1072-1085, http://www.piketty.pse.ens.fr/files/Baumol1986.pdf (accessed on 4 March 2021). [13]

Belinga, V. et al. (2014), "Tax Buoyancy in OECD Countries", https://doi.org/10.5089/9781498305075.001 (accessed on 14 April 2021). [1]

Delgado, F. (2013), "Are Taxes Converging in Europe? Trends and Some Insights into the Effect of Economic Crisis", https://doi.org/10.4172/2375-4389.1000102. [16]

Esteve, V., S. Sosvilla-Rivero and C. Tamarit (2000), "Convergence in fiscal pressure across EU countries", *Applied Economics Letters*, Vol. 7/2, pp. 117-123, https://doi.org/10.1080/135048500351942. [14]

Honohan, P. (2021), *Is Ireland really the most prosperous country in Europe?*, http://www.centralbank.ie (accessed on 24 February 2021). [19]

Johansson, Å. et al. (2008), *Tax and economic growth*, http://www.oecd.org/eco/working_papers (accessed on 14 September 2020). [9]

Kant, C. (2019), "Income convergence and the catch-up index", *North American Journal of Economics and Finance*, Vol. 48, pp. 613-627, https://doi.org/10.1016/j.najef.2018.07.017. [5]

Mankiw, N., D. Romer and D. Weil (1992), *A contribution to the empirics of economic growth*, https://academic.oup.com/qje/article/107/2/407/1838296 (accessed on 4 March 2021). [11]

OECD (2021), *OECD Secretary-General Tax Report to G20 finance ministers and central bank governors*, http://www.oecd.org/termsandconditions (accessed on 13 April 2021). [21]

OECD (2020), *Chile : Technical Assistance Report—Assessment of Tax Expenditures and Corrective Taxes*, https://www.imf.org/en/Publications/CR/Issues/2020/11/19/Chile-Technical-Assistance-Report-Assessment-of-Tax-Expenditures-and-Corrective-Taxes-49906 (accessed on 11 March 2021). [8]

OECD (2020), *Revenue Statistics 2020*, OECD Publishing, Paris, https://doi.org/10.1787/8625f8e5-en. [2]

OECD (2020), *Taxing Wages*, https://www.oecd-ilibrary.org/docserver/047072cd-en.pdf?expires=1615479568&id=id&accname=ocid84004878&checksum=5838DE790CB9D03C390BFB53799AC002 (accessed on 11 March 2021). [20]

OECD (2018), *OECD Economic Surveys: Chile 2018*, OECD Publishing, Paris, https://doi.org/10.1787/eco_surveys-chl-2018-en. [6]

OECD (2018), "Special feature: Convergence of tax levels and tax structures in OECD countries", in *Revenue Statistics 2018*, OECD Publishing, Paris, https://doi.org/10.1787/rev_stats-2018-5-en. [3]

OECD (2010), *OECD Tax Policy Studies Tax Policy Reform and Economic Growth no. 20.* [4]

OECD (2006), *Summary of a workshop on global convergence scenarios: structural and policy issues 3*, http://www.oecd.org/document/18/0,2340,en_2649_33733_35857618_1_1_1_1,00.html. (accessed on 16 December 2020). [7]

Quah, D. (1995), "Empirics for Economic Growth and Convergence", *European Economic Review*, Vol. Volume 40/Issue 6, pp. Pages 1353-1375, https://doi.org/10.1016/0014-2921(95)00051-8 (accessed on 14 January 2021). [17]

Rodrik, D. (2011), *The future of economic convergence*, National Bureau of Economic Research, https://doi.org/10.3386/w17400 (accessed on 15 December 2020). [15]

Tibulca (2015), "Is there evidence of tax convergence in the European Union?", *Procedia Economics and Finance*, Vol. 32, pp. 194-199, https://doi.org/10.1016/S2212-5671(15)01382-9. [12]

Notes

[1] OECD revenue statistics classify social security contributions (SSCs) as tax revenues. SSCs are similar to but not the same as tax revenues. Like taxes, SSCs are compulsory. Unlike taxes, SSC benefits can depend on SSC contributions having been made.

[2] PPP are currency converters that control for differences in price levels between countries, making it possible to compare absolute values across countries.

[3] Based on OECD population projection statistics.

[4] A weighted average of the countries in the OECD in a given year.

[5] According to the analysis in the cited in the above OECD Economic Survey of Chile 2018, the tax-to-GDP ratio rose from 20.2% in 2003 to 25.5% in 2007. When copper revenues are excluded over this period, the tax-to-GDP ratio fell from 19.2% to 17.3%.

[6] Under OECD Revenue Statistics, SSCs paid to the general government are classified as tax revenues. SSCs are similar to but not the same as tax revenues. Like taxes, SSCs are compulsory. Unlike taxes, SSC benefits can depend on SSC contributions having been made.

[7] The tax-to-GDP ratio in Chile is 20.7% in 2019 when SSCs are included and 19.6% when they are not. The tax-to-GDP ratio in the OECD is 33.9% in 2018 when SSCs are included and 24.9% when they are not. 2018 data are used for the OECD average because later data are not available for SSCs.

[8] As we have seen previously, while's tax-to-GDP has grown somewhat faster than that of the OECD since 1990 resulting in a reduction in the absolute tax-to-GDP gap from 14.2 in 1990 to 13.1 in 2019.

[9] Other strands define fiscal convergence as convergence toward the Maastricht criteria.

[10] Other measures also exist including gamma convergence, which measure changes in the ranking of economies over time.

[11] Heteroscedasticity is when the size of the error term differs across values of an independent variable.

[12] The latest year for which OECD revenue statistics data are available.

[13] As measured by GDP per capita.

www.ingramcontent.com/pod-product-compliance
Lightning Source LLC
Chambersburg PA
CBHW051235200326
41519CB00025B/7382